Beginner's Guide to Android App Development

A Practical Approach for Beginners

Serhan Yamacli

Manchester Academic
Publishers

Beginner's Guide to Android App Development – First Edition

This book is dedicated to my grandparents…

Table of Contents

BEGINNER'S GUIDE TO ANDROID APP DEVELOPMENT

INTRODUCTION

Welcome to your guide to Android™ app development!

This book aims to teach the basics of Android app development in Android Studio using Java programming language. I assume that you don't have any Java® or Android programming experience at the start of this book. I am going to explain every bit of app development in simple terms. You'll start from scratch and will be able to convert your ideas to your own apps after completing this book. A single book obviously cannot make you the best expert on a platform or programming language however you'll have a solid background and hands-on experience on Android app development with this book.

Android apps had been developed using Eclipse integrated development environment (IDE) with Android Development Tools (ADT) plugin in the past. However, Google introduced Android Studio as the official IDE for Android app development in 2014 and this IDE became the standard. The latest stable release is Android Studio 2.2, which will be used in this book.

Let's overview the fundamentals of Android operating system and the related concepts before starting our programming journey.

1.1. The Android Operating System

Android is an open-source mobile operating system. It is a variant of Linux hence providing extensive security, modularity and productivity at the mobile device level. Android is developed and maintained by the organization called "Open Headset Alliance" (OHA). OHA was established in 2007 with Google being its foremost member. OHA includes a lot of prominent hardware and software companies.

Originally, Android was created by a company called Android Inc. Google acquired this company in 2005. After then, Google made it open-source and Android gained a big momentum. Android has the market share of around 85% in 2016 as shown in Figure 1.1 (data source: http://www.idc.com/). Considering this market share, it is obviously rewarding to invest in Android app development.

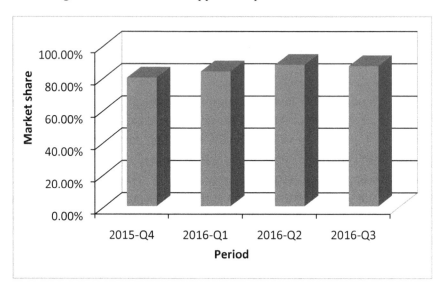

Figure 1.1. Market shares of mobile operating systems between 2015-Q4 and 2016-Q3

Android has seven major releases each having several minor revisions. In order to follow these versions easier, developers name them with cookie names. The popular versions of Android are Kitkat (Android 4.4), Lollipop (Android 5.1) and Marshmallow (Android 6.0) (https://www.statista.com/statistics/271774/share-of-android-platforms-on-mobile-devices-with-android-os/). Nougat (Android 7.0) is also gaining popularity. Android becomes more capable as the version goes up. However, we have to be careful about selecting the version during app development because not every device uses the latest version. If we develop an app for the Lollipop, it may not run on a device which has Froyo installed. Fortunately, Android Studio enables us to select set the compatibility.

Android is utilized not only in smartphones but also in tablets, netbooks, digital television boxes, handheld game devices and even in single board computers such as UDOO. Therefore we first need to select the target device(s) and version(s) before developing an app.

1.2. How do Android Apps Work?

There are different ways the programs run on various platforms. The lowest level software can be written in machine code that runs directly on the microprocessor. This is shown in Figure 1.2. Since it is difficult to develop complex applications in machine code, operating systems are used. Operating systems provide a communication and control layer between the application software and the hardware as shown in Figure 1.3. If we want to develop a native application for running on a specific hardware/operating system, we have to do this using a compiler and linker. Compiler and linker takes the source code and creates the executable file that actually runs on the operating system as shown in Figure 1.4. For example, if we want to develop an application in C++ programming language, we have to utilize the compilation/linking process.

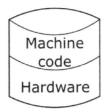

Figure 1.2. Machine code – hardware relation

The main advantage of native applications is their speed. However, the disadvantage is the incompatibility across different platforms. For example, we cannot run a native Windows application on Ubuntu and vice versa. Virtual machine concept is developed to overcome this limitation. Virtual machine is software that runs on the operating system and provides an abstraction to the developer as shown in Figure 1.5. The application software runs on top of the virtual machine.

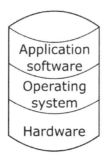

Figure 1.3. Operating system layer between the hardware and the app

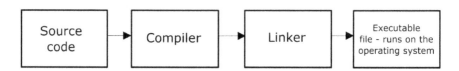

Figure 1.4. Creating a native executable from the source code

Therefore, as long as a computer has the virtual machine running, the application software can run on that computer independent of the hardware and the operating system. A good example is the Java Virtual Machine (JVM). JVM runs on almost all operating systems and platforms. Therefore, when we develop Java software, it will be run on the JVM independent of the operating system/platform.

The obvious advantage of developing apps that run on virtual machines can then be stated as: "develop once and run on all platforms". However, applications running on virtual machines are slower than native applications.

General development process of virtual machine applications is summarized in Figure 1.6.

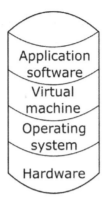

Figure 1.5. Virtual machine between the app and the operating system

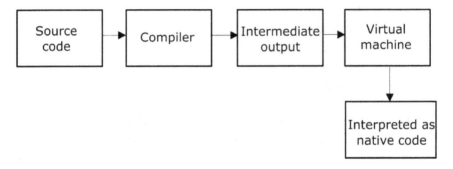

Figure 1.6. Creating an intermediate code from the source code – intermediate code is interpreted by the virtual machine

Similar to Java applications, Android applications also run on a JVM. There are two special virtual machines used in Android: Dalvik Virtual Machine (DVM) and Android RunTime (ART). These are specialized JVMs which can run on low system resources. The .apk files (executables of Android apps) actually run on these virtual machines. DVM has been the default runtime environment (~ virtual machine) until the Lollipop release (Android 5.0). ART is introduced by Android 4.0 and has been the default VM as of Android 5.0. DVM and ART basically do the same job: running Android apps independent of the platform. The main advantage of ART over DVM is the utilization of a concept called Ahead of Time (AOT) compilation instead of Just in Time (JIT) approach. In AOT, apps are compiled during installation hence they load faster with lower CPU usage. On the other hand, JIT compilation provides lower storage space consumption with relatively longer loading times.

1.3. Programming Languages Used For Developing Android Apps

The recommended and convenient way of developing Android apps is using Java programming language. Although Java is a general purpose tool, it is used in conjunction with Android Software Development Kit (SDK) in Android Studio environment to develop apps. Another official way is using C++ with the Native Development Kit (NDK). This option is used for developing apps with low level instructions such as timing sensitive drivers. With C++ and NDK, we can directly run the app on the Android kernel hence increasing efficiency in exchange of code length and development cost. There also exist third-party tools like Xamarin, Crodova and React Native for developing apps. These platforms provide convenience however a native-like performance isn't normally expected from the apps developed by third party tools.

We'll use the standard and official way of developing Android apps: Java with Android SDK and we'll use Android Studio Integrated Development Environment (IDE) for this job. You don't need to know Java to start following this book because the basics of Java are also explained in Chapter 4.

I'll not introduce complicated subjects until I'm sure that you understand the basics because it is very easy to get lost while learning a new programming language. You'll not be in such a situation with this book. I'll try to teach new concepts in the simplest way possible. Please don't forget that learning a programming language is a non-stop process, it never ends and this book will help you get started easily.

Now, you know the aims and the method of this book. Let's continue with installation of the Android Studio in the next chapter after having a coffee break.

SETTING UP YOUR DEVELOPMENT ENVIRONMENT

We'll use Android Studio, which is the official IDE for Android app development; therefore we need to install it with the required plugins.

2.1. Installation of Android Studio

Android Studio runs on Java Runtime Environment (JRE). JRE can be installed on Windows, Mac and Linux computers. We need to follow the steps given below for the installation of Android Studio independent of our operating system:

1. Installation of Java: Java is developed by Oracle Inc. There are basically two Java packages: Java Runtime Environment (JRE) and Java Software Development Kit (JDK). JRE is used for running software written in Java programming language whereas JDK is utilized for developing Java software. Therefore, installing JRE is adequate for running Android Studio because we will not develop Java software here.

Please navigate to the following website to download the JRE: http://www.oracle.com/technetwork/java/javase/downloads/jre8-downloads-2133155.html. You'll be presented with the download options shown in Figure 2.1. Just select the version compatible with your operating system, download it and install it with the usual installation procedure (Next, next, ...).

2. Installation of Android Studio and Android SDK

Android Studio is bundled with Android Software Development Kit (SDK). Please navigate to the official download site located at:

https://developer.android.com/studio/index.html . The download link for the Windows version is shown at the top of this site but if you scroll down, you can find the setup files available for download for other operating systems as shown in Figure 2.2.

Figure 2.1. Download options for Java Runtime Environment

Select a different platform

Platform	Android Studio package	Size	SHA-1 checksum
Windows (64-bit)	android-studio-bundle-145.3537739-windows.exe Includes Android SDK (recommended)	1.674 MB (1,756,130,200 bytes)	272105b119adbcababa114abeee4c78f3001bcf7
	android-studio-ide-145.3537739-windows.exe No Android SDK	417 MB (437,514,160 bytes)	b52c0b25c85c252fe55056d40d5b1a40a1ccd03c
	android-studio-ide-145.3537739-windows.zip No Android SDK, no installer	438 MB (460,290,402 bytes)	8c9fe06aac4be3ead5e500f27ac53543edc055e1
Windows (32-bit)	android-studio-ide-145.3537739-windows32.zip No Android SDK, no installer	438 MB (459,499,381 bytes)	59fba5a17a508533b0decde584849b213fa39c65
Mac	android-studio-ide-145.3537739-mac.dmg	434 MB (455,263,302 bytes)	51f282234c3a78b4afc084d8ef43660129332c37
Linux	android-studio-ide-145.3537739-linux.zip	438 MB (459,957,542 bytes)	172c9b01669f2fe46edcc16e466917fac04c9a7f

Figure 2.2. Download options for Android Studio

When you download and install Android Studio, Android SDK will also be automatically installed.

3. Installation of SDK updates: After the installation of Android Studio, it is better to check SDK updates. For this, run Android Studio and open the SDK manager from Tools → Android → SDK Manager as shown below:

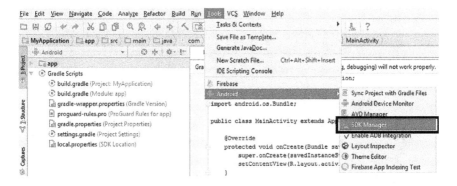

Figure 2.3. Opening the SDK Manager

The SDK Manager window will appear as shown in Figure 2.4.

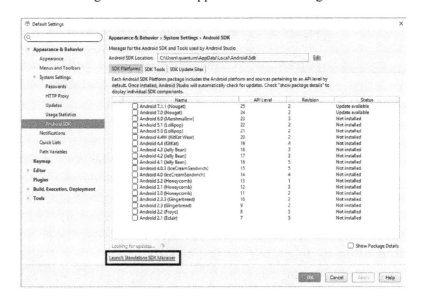

Figure 2.4. Android SDK Manager

Please open the standalone SDK Manager by clicking the link indicated in Figure 2.4. In the standalone SDK Manager, click on the "Install … packages" as shown below:

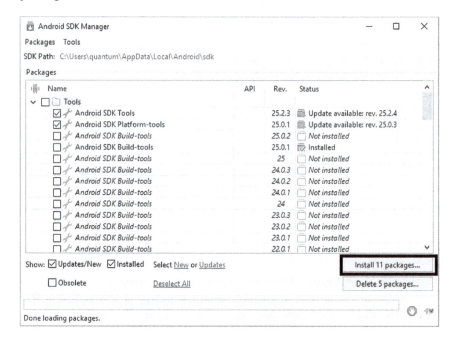

Figure 2.5. Standalone SDK Manager

After you install the packages, you'll have the latest SDK and be ready to develop apps. However, before our test drive app one more step is needed: setting up the emulators.

2.2. Installation of Emulators

Emulators are software that mimics the behaviour of real devices. When we develop an app, we obviously won't have all the possible devices (Android phones, tablets, etc.) available at hand. Because of this, we run the apps on emulators for testing on various devices. Emulators are also called as "Android Virtual Devices (AVDs)" in Android Studio. When Android Studio is first installed, there is no default AVD. We need to create one before testing our apps. For this, select Tools → Android → AVD Manager as shown in Figure 2.6.

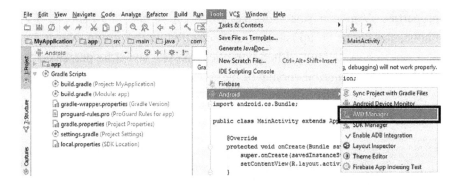

Figure 2.6 Launching the AVD Manager

When AVD Manager appears, there won't be any AVDs created or installed. Please click on the + **Create a Virtual Device** button as shown below:

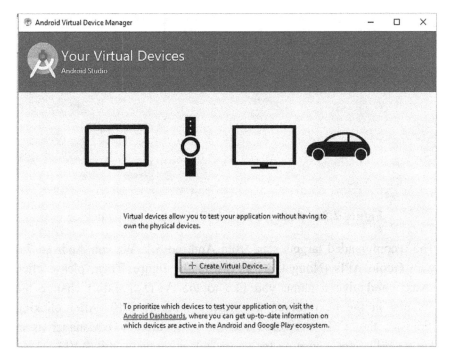

Figure 2.7. Creating a new AVD

AVD Manager will show a detailed window as in Figure 2.8. You can select various devices with different screen sizes and other hardware properties. You can select device groups from the left pane as TV, Phone, etc. Phone group is the default selection. In this group, Nexus 5 is also selected by default. When you click "Next", you'll be presented by choices for the Android version of the AVD as shown in Figure 2.9.

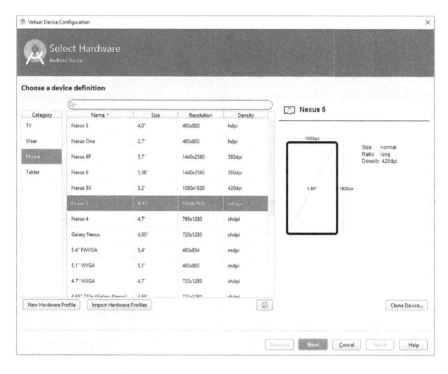

Figure 2.8. Creating a new AVD – selecting the device

The recommended targets start from Android 5.1. We can Android 7.0 with Goole APIs (Nougat) as shown in the figure. Then, please click "Next" and give a name you like to the AVD. I didn't change the defaults in the next screen as shown in Figure 2.10. After clicking "Finish", the AVD is created and shown in the AVD Manager as in Figure 2.11. You can now try your Android apps on this AVD, which will accurately mimic the behaviour of a real Nexus 5 phone.

We can run the AVD by clicking the "Play" button shown inside the square in Figure 2.11. The virtual device will appear as in Figure 2.12 which you can use like a real Nexus 5 phone.

After installing both the development environment and the emulator, we're now ready to develop our test drive app, Hello World, in the next chapter.

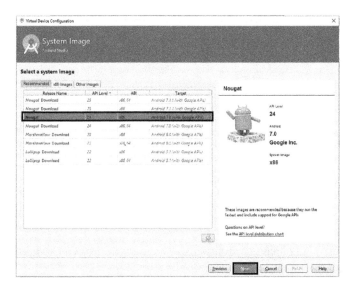

Figure 2.9. Selecting the Android version of the AVD

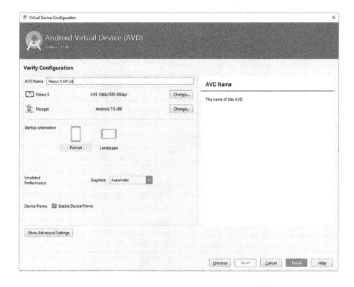

Figure 2.10. Final settings of the AVD

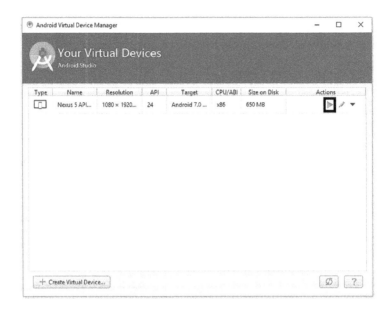

Figure 2.11. Newly created AVD shown in the AVD Manager

Figure 2.12. Nexus 5 emulator window

TEST DRIVE: THE HELLO WORLD APP

3.1. General Procedure for Developing an App

A good method for testing the installation of a compiler or a development environment is to try a "Hello World" example. It just displays a text such as "Hello World" on the screen. OK, I know it is not an app that you'd be proud of showing to your family or friends but its usefulness stems from testing whether your programming environment is working properly and to see if you're ready to go for real projects. In our very first Android project, we will develop an app in which the "Hello, World!" text will be shown in the middle of the device screen. We will test it on the emulator we created before but if you have access to an Android device, you can test your "Hello World" app on it too.

I'd like to point out general steps of app development before setting off for developing our first app:

1. Creating an Android Studio project,

2. Setting up the User Interface (UI) of the app,

3. Connecting the UI components such as buttons, textboxes, etc. to the Java code,

4. Coding in Java – the actual programming part

5. Building the project: this means creating the executable (file that actually runs on device or the emulator). This is not difficult as it sounds; Android Studio does the entire job with a single click,

6. Trying the app on an emulator,

7. Running the app on a real Android device (optional),

8. Publishing the app on Google Play (optional).

3.2. Creating a New Android Studio Project

When we run Android Studio for the first time, we are presented by the dialog shown in Figure 3.1 where several options are available: i) Start a new Android Project, ii) Open an existing project, iii) Check out a project from a version control website (like GitHub), iv) Import a project created in a different development environment (like Eclipse) or v) Import an Android code sample (where code samples are downloaded from version control websites). We'll develop our first Android project therefore please select the first option shown by the arrow in Figure 3.1.

Figure 3.1. Creating a new Android Studio project for our first app

After selecting to create a new project, a dialog box for entering the project settings will appear as in Figure 3.2. In the first textbox (shown by "1" in the figure), we are required to enter the project name, which will also be the name of the app. I entered "Hello World" but you can enter another name as you wish. The company domain is given in the next textbox shown by "2". This is a string similar to a web address that is used to distinguish among developers in the Google Play market. You can use any unique domain here. If you won't upload your app to Google Play (as in this example where we're just developing for learning the basics), you can use any domain you like. I used the one shown in the figure. And then, we need to select the location on the computer to save the project files (shown by "3"). You can select any place you like to save your project files.

Figure 3.2. New project settings

After clicking "Next", the Target Android Devices window shown in Figure 3.3 will appear. I selected the Phone and Tablet checkbox and then set the Minimum SDK as API 15 – Android 4.0.3. This means that the app we'll develop will be able to run on devices having Android version 4.0.3 or higher. After selecting the target, please click "Next".

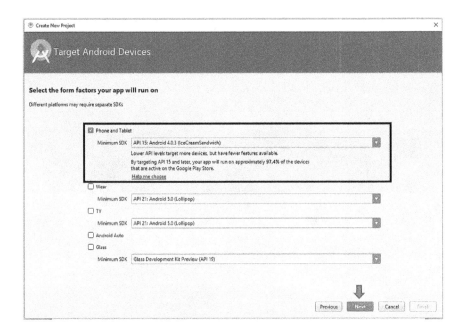

Figure 3.3. Selecting target devices

The template of the user interface is selected in the following dialog. As you can see from Figure 3.4, there are several templates including a login activity, maps activity, etc. However, since our aim is just writing a text on the screen, it is OK to select the Empty Activity as shown in Figure 3.4. So, what does an **activity** mean? **Activities can be defined as screens shown to the user with user interfaces.** Therefore, we have to include an activity to have an app because as you know Android apps are visual programs that have one or more user interfaces.

After selecting the default activity, Android Studio asks us to give names to the activity and the related layout file as shown in Figure 3.5. Since we will have a single activity in this app, it is perfectly OK to leave their names as defaults. When we click "Finish", Android Studio will create the project files and folders automatically (this make take a while) and then the IDE will appear as in Figure 3.6.

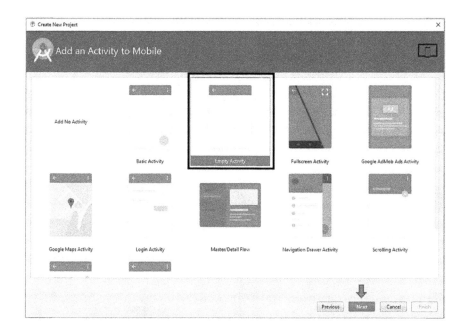

Figure 3.4. Adding an activity template to the app

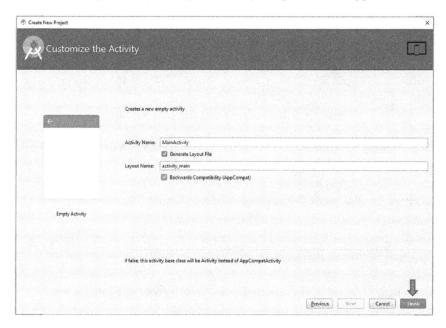

Figure 3.5. Customizing the newly added activity

3.3. Main Sections of the IDE

Android Studio is a sophisticated tool therefore it has dozens of properties to make app development easier. Instead of giving every detail of this IDE at once, I prefer to explain and teach in a slower way so that the reader can grasp the app development concepts in a solid way. Let's start with explaining the main sections of Android Studio by referring to Figure 3.6.

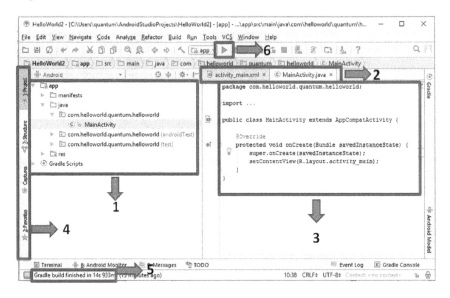

Figure 3.6. Basics sections of Android Studio

The sections of Android Studio in the figure above can be summarized as follows:

Section 1. The project files and folders can be viewed from here. In addition, new files can be added from this pane. We need to double-click on the filenames here to open them in the middle pane. The project structure will be explained in detail in the next subsection.

Section 2. The opened files can be activated from the tabs located here for viewing in the middle pane.

Section 3. This is the middle pane. Contents of the active files can be viewed and changed from here. For the project shown in Figure 3.6, the file called "MainActivity.java" is the active tab in Section 2 therefore the middle pane in Section 3 shows the contents of this "MainActivity.java" file.

Section 4. This section is also controlled via tabs. The developer can switch project files, structures, captures and favourites for viewing in the left pane.

Section 5. The current or previous compilation, building or debugging processes are shown here. For the snapshot of Figure 3.6, it is indicated that the "Gradle build finished in 14 seconds". Gradle is the build system of Android Studio. Therefore, the message says that the building engine completed its previous task in 14 seconds.

Section 6. This is the **Run** button of Android Studio. When we set up the user interface and write the Java code of a project, we click this button to make the Android Studio build the project (which means creating the executable file from project files) and then we can run it on an emulator or on a real device.

3.4. Folder and File Structure of an Android Studio Project

The file structure of an Android project can be viewed in various forms in Android Studio. The button just at above the left pane (shown by the arrow) is used to open the selection box for choosing the preferred method of viewing the file hierarchy as shown in Figure 3.7. The default file viewer is the "Android" mode which is the easiest way of grouping files and folders in my opinion. When the selection is the "Android" mode, the default files and folders shown in Figure 3.8 is shown in the left pane. You can use the arrows (shown inside the circle in the figure) for viewing the contents of folders.

The default folders (shown inside the rectangles in Figure 3.8) and their contents are explained as follows:

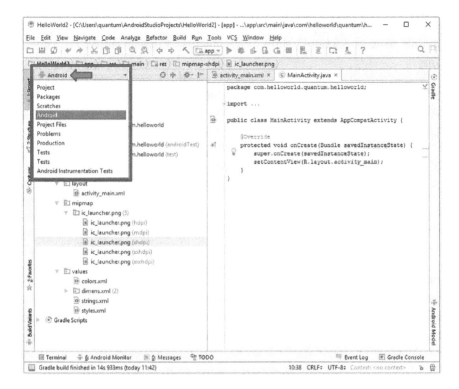

Figure 3.7. Switching among different ways of viewing files and folders

1. manifests folder: This folder has the AndroidManifest.xml file inside. This file contains the configuration parameters of the project such as permissions, services and additional libraries.

2. java folder: The source code files written in Java programming language reside in this folder. You can see that the java file of the activity named "MainActivity.java" is automatically created in this folder.

3. res folder: The resource files are contained in this folder. Resources basically mean all the needed files except the source code. For example, if we want to include an mp3 file in our project, we place this file inside the "res" folder.

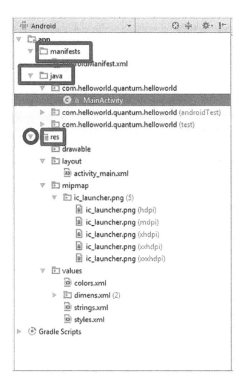

Figure 3.8. Default folder and file structure of an Android project

The media, image and layout files residing in the resources folder are accessed via Java code written in MainActivity.java as we'll see in a while.

3.5. Building the User Interface

Android Studio provides an easy way of designing user interfaces. The file named "activity_main.xml" located under the "res/layout" folder contains all the layout information of the current activity.

If we try to open an .xml file outside of Android Studio, it is opened by a text editor or a browser. However, when we open an .xml file in Android Studio, it reads the .xml file and shows the corresponding activity layout with its components. In order to open the activity_main.xml in Android Studio, please double-click on it in the project explorer and the activity layout will be displayed in the middle pane as shown below:

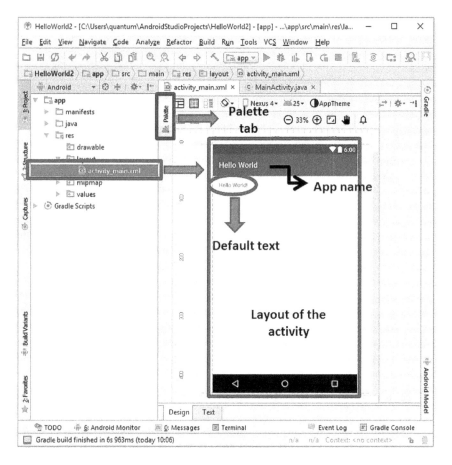

Figure 3.9. Layout of the activity

As you can see, the layout of the activity is shown in the middle pane. The name of the app appears at the top of the activity. The default empty activity contains a default text which is shown inside the circle in the above figure. At the left top of the middle pane, there exists a tab called "Palette" indicated inside the rectangle in the figure. When we click on this tab, the palette shown in Figure 3.10 appears from which we can add all possible user interface objects and layout templates to the activity.

Figure 3.10. The component palette

When the palette tab is clicked, two panes are opened: the Palette shown by the upper rectangle and the Component Tree pane inside the lower rectangle in Figure 3.10.

The Palette contains several groups like Widgets, Text Fields and Layouts. We can easily drag and drop these components to the user interface. On the other hand, the Component Tree lists the activity's components in a hierarchical manner. We'll see the utilization of these components as we develop complex apps in the following chapters. However, our aim for now is to write a text on the screen. As you can see from Figure 3.10, Android Studio already placed a "Hello World" text at the top left of the view.

Let's position this text, comprised of a **TextView** widget, to the middle of the view. For this, select this TextView and then drag and drop to the middle by the help of the guiding lines as shown below:

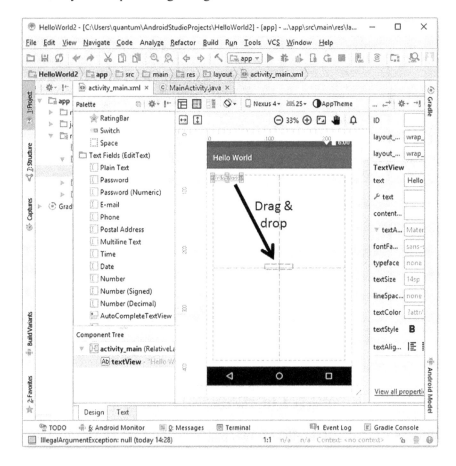

Figure 3.11. Drag and drop operation on the TextView

After the drag and drop operation, the TextView will be kept selected. We can now change the properties of the TextView using the Properties pane which is at the right of the Layout view as shown inside the rectangle in Figure 3.12. Please click the arrow shown inside the circle in this figure to open the basic editable properties of the TextView.

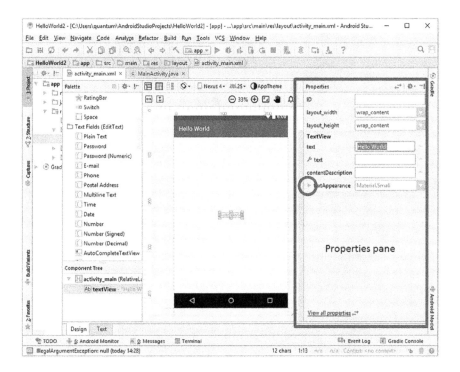

Figure 3.12. The Properties pane

The editable properties of the TextView component are shown inside the rectangle in Figure 3.13. In order to display the "Hello World" text in a better way, I changed its text size to 24sp (sp = scale–independent pixels) and its style to bold by clicking the **B** button in the textStyle section.

We have now completed setting up the user interface. Since we don't want our first app to do something interactive, we don't need to write single line of code for now. Of course we'll do a lot of coding in the upcoming projects but we don't need any coding here.

3.6. Building the Project and Running on an Emulator

Our first Android app is now ready to be run on an emulator. This is easy in Android Studio. We have set up a Nexus 5 emulator in the previous chapter therefore the only things we need to do are i) building the project, ii) selecting the emulator and then, iii) run our app on the emulator.

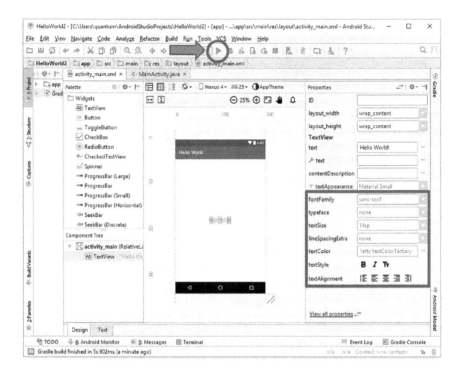

Figure 3.13. The editable properties of the TextView

In order to build and run the project, please click the "Run" button as indicated by the arrow in Figure 3.13. The emulator and device selection dialog shown in Figure 3.14 will appear. Since we have created a Nexus 5 emulator before, it is automatically selected as shown inside the rectangle. If we had connected a real Android device via USB cable to the computer, it would also show up in this dialog. However, since there is no real device connected for now, the dialog gives a warning at the top shown inside the ellipse in the figure. Please click "Next" and then the emulator will boot like a real device. It takes some time depending on your computer speed to completely start the emulator (something like 20 secs).

When the emulator starts running, you'll see a Nexus 5 screen as shown in Figure 3.15. You can use it like a real device (apart from calling and SMS features of course☺), and you can also use the controls on the right bar for changing general properties of the emulator if you want to.

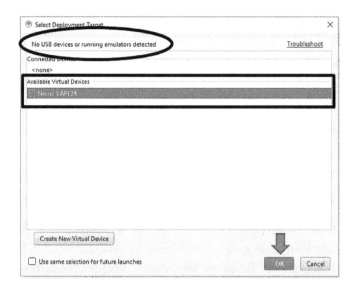

Figure 3.14. Selecting the target for running our first app

Figure 3.15. The Nexus 5 emulator

The emulator started but we cannot see our app running on it. Don't panic! If we check the main Android Studio window, we can see that it has given a warning as shown below:

Figure 3.16. Instant Run warning

Android Studio asks us if we want to utilize a component called Instant Run. Instant Run is a system introduced in Android Studio 2.0 and it shortens the Code → Build → Run cycle. When we use Instant Run, Android Studio pushes code updates to the emulator without the need of building a new executable. Therefore, viewing the effects of the changes of the code can be seen on the emulator in a shorter time. In summary, Instant Run is a good thing so let's install it by clicking the "Install and Continue" button shown in Figure 3.16. Android Studio will download the required files in a short time, and then we need to install these updates by the usual next-next procedure. After the tiny installation, Android Studio will build our project as indicated inside the rectangle in Figure 3.17.

After the building process, the emulator will run our first app as in Figure 3.18. **If you see the emulator screen shown in this figure, congratulations. You've successfully created your first Android app.**

We can make any change in our app, and then press the "Re-Run" button indicated by the arrow in Figure 3.19. The emulator will install the updated app for emulating.

As you can see from your very first project, Android Studio offers vast number of possibilities and a user–friendly interface for transforming your ideas into Android apps.

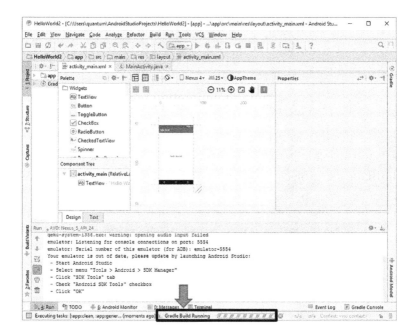

Figure 3.17. Android Studio in the process of building our project

Figure 3.18. Emulator running our "Hello World" app

Figure 3.19. The "Re-Run" button in Android Studio

I changed the text to "Hello Android!" from the TextView properties pane (shown in Figure 3.12) and pressed the Re-Run button. Android Studio built the project again and the updated app is displayed on the emulator screen as below:

Figure 3.20. The emulator running the updated app

You can stop the emulator running the app using the square red "Stop" button which is just at the right of the "Re-Run" button. When you stop the app, the emulator will not shut down completely and wait for the next run.

3.7. Running on a Real Device

It is also easy to try our app on a real Android device.

1. Things to be done on the device: Before running/debugging apps on the real device, we have to enable the Developer Mode on the device. For this, on your real device please navigate to Settings → About → Build number **or** Settings → About →Software information → Build number. Depending on your device and Android version, **the place of the "Build number" may be different** however I'm sure you can find it easily in the Settings → About section. Once you find the **Build number**, tap on it **seven times** and then your device will show a dialog box saying "You're now a developer."

After you've enabled the Developer Mode, you'll find a new section called "Developer options" under the Settings of your device. Please tap on it and then check "USB debugging" to enable debugging via the USB connection. You can now install apps from Android Studio to your device over the usual USB connection.

2. Things to be done in Android Studio: First of all, please enable "ADB Integration" from Tools → Android → ADB Integration as shown below:

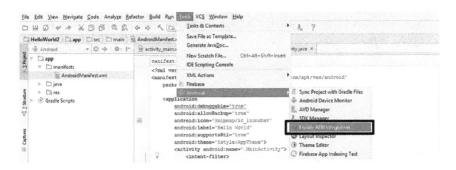

Figure 3.21. Enabling ADB Integration in Android Studio

Now, we need to make our app "debuggable". For this, open the AndroidManifest.xml file by double-clicking on it and add the text

```
android:debuggable="true"
```
Code 3.1

inside the <application> element as shown in Figure 3.22.

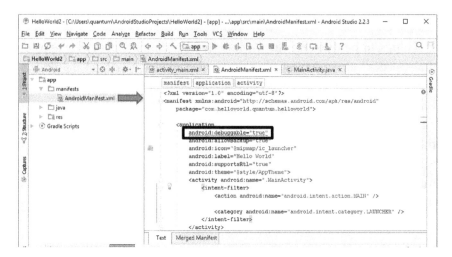

Figure 3.22. Adding the "debuggable" property to our app

We are now ready to test our "Hello World" app on the real device. When we hit the "Run" button in Android Studio, the following device selection window will appear:

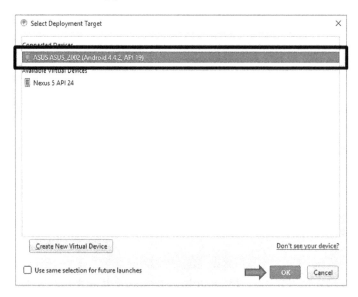

Figure 3.23. Selecting the real device

I have connected my Asus Zenfone 6 hence its name is written in the device selection window; it will obviously be different if the device you connected is different. After the device selection, click on the "OK" button and then the app screen of Figure 3.18 should appear on your actual device. If you see the "Hello World!" text on the real device, it's excellent. You now know how to install your apps on real Android devices. Running an app on a real hardware is sometimes essential because some operations like SMS sending and calling can only be done on real devices.

We have developed out test drive app, "Hello World", and learned

i) Creating an Android Studio project,

ii) Using user interfaces and widgets,

iii) Creating emulators,

iv) Building the app,

v) Running our app on the emulator,

vi) Running our app on a real device.

But as you may have noticed, we didn't have any interaction with our app. It just writes a text on the screen and that's it. In order to make an app to do something, we need to program it. Java is the main programming language used for developing Android apps. We'll learn the basics of Java in the next chapter which will enable us to transform our ideas to working Android apps. Let's have a coffee break (a 3in1 coffee is recommended since we'll need glucose) before starting our Java lecture.

JAVA BASICS

4.1. What is Java?

We have developed our first app. That's great. However, it just writes a text on the screen and that's it. The user doesn't have any interaction with our app. In order to make an app to be interactive and do something real, we need to tell it what to do. And we need to tell it exactly. We do this by using programming languages.

As an old saying states: "Computers are actually rather stupid". This is because: **if we're telling a computer to do a task, then we have to do this in exact terms.** Let's try to explain this by an example: imagine that you had a tiring workday and going home with your stomach rumbling. While you're on the way on M4 motorway, the traffic got crowded near Oxford and you had some time to think what you'll have for the dinner. You suddenly remembered that there is frozen chicken korma in the fridge. You ring your wife (with hands–free of course!) and will ask her to cook that meal.

You – Hi darling, hope you're OK.

Your wife – Thanks, a bit tired. You?

You – Me too. And also very hungry. Could you please cook a frozen chicken korma for me? There should be some in the fridge. I'm sure you'll also have one, I know you love it.

Your partner – Yummy yummy. I'll darling, it will be sizzling when you arrive. See you in a while, bye. (A caring wife!)

You – Thanks darling, bye.

Then, she'll find the frozen korma wherever it is in the fridge, unpack it, remove the sleeve and pierce film lid in several places. Set the timer, power on the microwave (or oven) and cook it. She'll cook the included pilau rice too without a need to ask you. That's it. However, if you had a robot wife with a computer brain, the dialog would be more like this:

You – Hi darling, hope you're OK.

Robot wife – Thanks. You OK? (not in a romantic tone!)

You – Very tired. And also very hungry. Could you please cook a frozen chicken korma for me? There should be some in the fridge.

Robot wife – Where is the frozen korma in fridge, do you want me to cook pilau rice too? Do you want them normal or overcooked? Do you want a garlic bread too? When do you want it to be ready?....

You – Stop, stop please. I'll drive to a restaurant.

Robot wife – I don't understand, you are nonsense....

Well, any programmable digital device is more or less the same. **We have to tell exact things to them.** We do this by using programming languages. There are a lot of different programming languages used to develop software for different platforms. You can check the widely used programming languages and their rankings at the TIOBE index website: http://www.tiobe.com/tiobe-index/. It is sometimes difficult to choose which programming language to use. There is not a universally excellent/complete programming language; they have strong and weak sides.

When we check the TIOBE index, we see that Java is consistently the most widely used programming language for years. There are several reasons for this. The main reasons are: i) being platform independence, ii) having a lot of libraries and iii) having object oriented nature, iv) having a strong security and robustness. Because of these reasons, Android apps are also mainly developed in Java. Therefore, in order to learn Android app development, we have to grasp the basics of Java programming language. After learning Java, we'll use Android SDK libraries with Java and develop Android apps.

We can use standalone Java compilers or Java-specific IDEs for learning Java. However it is also possible to try Java code in Android Studio with a simple trick. Since we already set up Android Studio, we will use it for Java coding here.

4.2. Using Android Studio for Java Coding

First of all, we need to launch Android Studio and create an Android project as we did in the previous chapter. We can name the project as we want and select any Android version and any screen layout for now. When the project loads, the project files and folders will be like the following in the left pane of Android Studio:

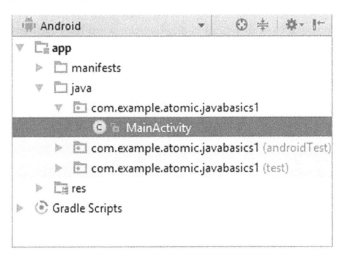

Figure 4.1. Default file structure of a new Android Studio project

We'll create a new Java file in order to try Java codes. For this, right click on one of the java folders such as **com.example.atomic.javabasics1** in the above figure (or another Java folder in the project you created, your folder names will be different because your project name is different) and then select New → Java Class as shown in Figure 4.2.

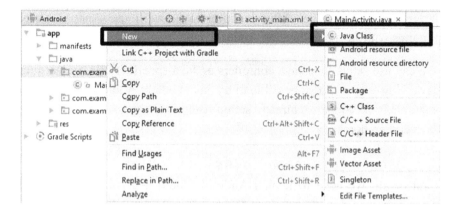

Figure 4.2. Creating a new Java Class

In Java, all programs are classes therefore we create a new Java Class. (We'll learn classes later in this chapter.) Please name the new class without any spaces and special characters (I named it as **JavaBasics**) and then click "OK" as shown below:

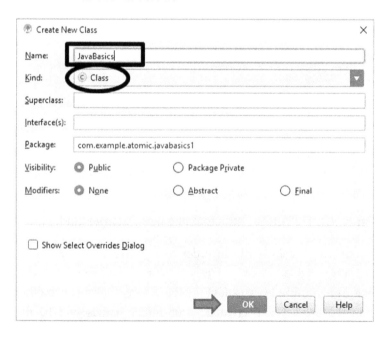

Figure 4.3. Creating a new Java file (Java class)

It is worth noting that the file kind is **class** as shown inside the ellipse in Figure 4.3. After clicking "OK", Android Studio will create the new Java file called **JavaBasics.java** and show it in the middle pane as shown in Figure 4.4.

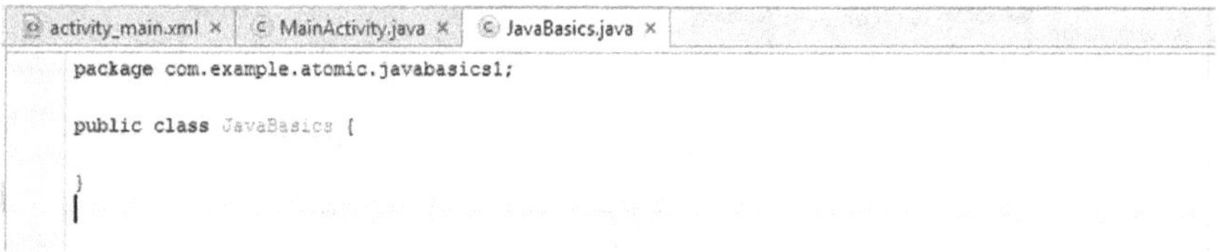

```
activity_main.xml ×    MainActivity.java ×    JavaBasics.java ×

    package com.example.atomic.javabasics1;

    public class JavaBasics {

    }

```

Figure 4.4. The contents of the new Java file

The new Java file has the following default lines of code:

```
package com.example.atomic.javabasics1;

public class JavaBasics {

}
```
Code 4.1

The first line defines a **package** that contains our new Java class. Java classes are organized in packages. Packages are like folders on your computer that hold several files inside.

The second line is the main **class** definition. All programs are classes in Java hence all Java files (programs) should have a class definition for compilation. Please always remember that **the class definition should match the name of the Java file** (in our case the filename is JavaBasics.java and the class name is JavaBasics).

The contents of the programs are written inside the curly brackets opened just after the class name definition in the second line and closed in the third line in Code 4.1.

Our Java file only has basic package and class definitions by default. The body of the Java class is empty thus this Java program does not do anything at all when it is compiled and run.

✓ The source files of Java programs have .java extension. The Java compiler generates a .class file from .java file. This .class file is then executed on a Java Virtual Machine. This flow is shown below:

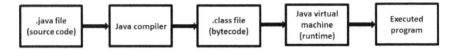

Figure 4.5. Compilation and execution of a Java program

Anyway, let's see how we can make a "Hello World" program from our JavaBasics.java file. In a Java source file, the following code line prints a text in the **terminal window**:

```
System.out.println("the text to be printed");
```
Code 4.2

In this code line, **System.out** means that Java will output something and **println()** method outputs the text written inside it. It is worth noting that texts are written inside double quotation marks ("...") so that the Java system knows that the programmer refers to a text. Therefore, by placing "Hello World" inside the function shown in Code 4.2, we can print "Hello World" text on the screen in Java using the code below:

```
System.out.println("Hello World");
```
Code 4.3

So, where will we place this line in our java file? We learned that the Java code should be between the curly brackets of the class definition. Hence, we may try to obtain our Java "Hello World" program by placing Code 4.3 into Code 4.1 as follows:

```
package com.example.atomic.javabasics1;

public class JavaBasics {

    System.out.println("Hello World");
}
```
Code 4.4

If we try to compile and run this code, the compiler gives an error and doesn't run our program. It is because **all Java programs should have a main method.** The **main** method indicates the starting point of a Java program which will be executed firstly when the program is run. Adding the main function, we obtain a correct "Hello World" program in Java as follows:

```
package com.example.atomic.javabasics1;

public class JavaBasics {

    public static void main(String args[]) {

    System.out.println("Hello World");
    }

}
```
Code 4.5

The main function is defined in line 3 above: `public static void main(String args[])`. In general, the **main** method is not explained at this stage and the tutors say "just accept the main method as it is for now, we'll learn more about it later". However, I'd like to point out the general structure of the **main** method:

This method has three keywords in the front: `public, static` and `void`. Their meanings can be summarized as follows:

1. `public`: the **main** method will be accessible from anywhere,

2. `static`: the **main** method doesn't belong to a specific object and

3. `void`: the **main** method will not return a value.

These will be clearer when we learn classes in the last subsection of this chapter.

The main method also has arguments which are the inputs to this method in the form of `String args[]`. These mean that the main method can have several inputs (arguments) in text form. These will be understood better when we dive deep on functions and their arguments later.

➢ Please don't panic and don't be put off at this point. I know these may be confusing and you might say "Writing just a Hello World program takes ages with Java and it is confusing." Java codes are generally longer compared to other programming languages. However, this is also a strong side of Java. This is because Java is a very organized and structured language that provides the developer with many possibilities with less error-prone coding.

After inserting Code 4.5 to our JavaBasics.java file, we are now ready to run our Java "Hello World" program. For this, find the JavaBasics.java from your file explorer in Android Studio, right-click on it and then select Run 'JavaBasics.main()' as shown below:

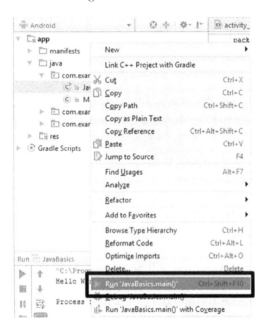

Figure 4.6. Running our Java program in Android Studio

Android Studio will compile our JavaBasics.java file and then run it. This takes a while. After then, the output of the program will be displayed in the Terminal window at the bottom pane of Android Studio as shown in Figure 4.7.

We have now written, compiled and run our first Java application in Android Studio without the need of using any other development environment. Let's continue with learning about variables used in Java in the next subsection.

Figure 4.7. Terminal output of our Java program in Android Studio

4.3. Variables in Java

Variables are entities that contain information. Variables can be thought as boxes that hold data. The creation of variables is called "the declaration of the variable" and placing its value during its declaration is referenced as "initializing the variable". We can insert the value of the variable during the declaration or later, depending on conditions.

Just as real world boxes that can be used to hold different things like a sugar box, a match box or a component box, variables in programming languages also have different types.

Java is defined as a statically and strongly typed programming language which means that the type of a variable should be defined during its creation and this type cannot be changed later. There are two variable type groups in Java:

1. Primitive variable types: These variable types hold single data at a time. In other words, primitive variables hold primitive values. Primitive variables always have values. Primitive variables exist from their creation to the end of a Java program.

2. Reference variable types: These "non-primitive" types are dynamic variables; they can be created and erased before the program ends. These variables store the addresses of objects they refer to. Unlike primitive types, reference types may have the value **null**, which means non-existence. The **null** value means the absence of its value.

These may seem confusing at first but please just try to remember that primitive types are used to store actual values but reference types store a handle to an object.

The widely used variable types used in Java are shown in the following figure:

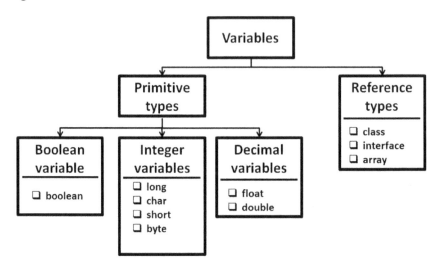

Figure 4.8. Variable types in Java

Let's explain the primitive data types first.

1. Boolean variables: Boolean variables have the property of having only two distinct values: `true` or `false`. We can think booleans as a yes–no question like "Is the screen background blue?" The answer can only be "yes" or "no". Instead of the words "yes" or "no", Java uses `true` or `false`. The following code defines a Boolean variable called `myBoolean` and assigns `true` as its value during the declaration:

```
boolean myBoolean = true;
```
Code 4.6

In this code, the word `boolean` is the keyword used for defining a boolean variable. The name of the variable to be created is written next to the keyword. In this example, the variable name is `myBoolean`. The equal sign (=) is used to assign a value therefore `true` is assigned to the newly created variable in this code. This assignment can be visualised as in Figure 4.9.

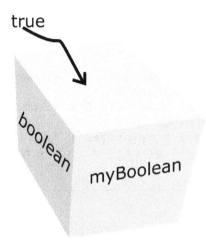

Figure 4.9. Assigning `true` to the variable myBoolean

On the other hand, Java statements are ended using a semicolon (`;`) as in Code 4.5 otherwise the compiler gives an error and doesn't compile our program. The template is similar for other variable types too. Boolean variables are generally utilized for decision making in applications which uses complex logic.

2. Integer variables: Integer variables are widely used in Java. An integer variable basically stores an integer value (a whole number that doesn't have fractional part). As it can be seen from Figure 4.8, integer variables have several forms: `int`, `long`, `short`, `char` and `byte`. Let's see what these types are used for:

❖   `int` type variables are used to store integer numbers. For example, the following code defines an integer and assigns the value of 5 to it during declaration. In other words, a new `int` type variable is created and initialized to 5:

```
int myInteger = 5;
```
Code 4.7

As you can see from this code, variables that hold integer numbers are defined using the keyword `int`. After defining and initializing an `int`, we can perform mathematical operations on it. The following code shows the whole Java source code where an `int` type variable is created, initialized and then another integer value is added to it before printing the result on the terminal screen:

```
package com.helloworld.quantum.helloworld;
public class JavaBasics {
    public static void main(String args[]){
        int myInteger = 5;
        myInteger = myInteger + 7;
        System.out.print("Sum = " + myInteger);
    }
}
```
Code 4.8

Let's analyse what happens in the above code:

➢ An `int` variable called `myInteger` is created and initialized to 5 on the fourth line.
➢ In the fifth line, this variable is added to the number 7 and then the result is assigned back to `myInteger` by the line `myInteger = myInteger + 7;` as shown below:

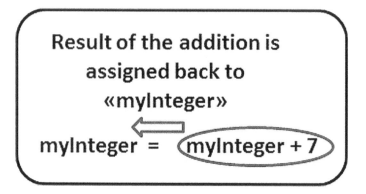

Figure 4.10. Addition principle

➢ Finally, the sixth line `System.out.print("Sum = " + myInteger);` prints out the value of `myInteger`.

Please note that, its value will be written next to the expression "`Sum = `" in this code. This Java program and its output are shown in Figure 4.11.

More arithmetic and logic operations can be applied on integer variables as we'll learn in our Android projects in the upcoming chapters.

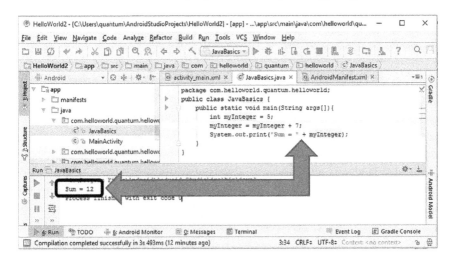

Figure 4.11. `int` type definition and addition operation in Java

❖ `int` type variables can store numbers from –2 147 483 648 to +2 147 483 647 (these are not phone numbers!). If the numbers we will use are not that big, we can use `short` type variables which have the limits of –32768 to +32767. If you say that you'll store numbers for rocket science, you can use `long` type variables instead, which have the range of -2^{63} to $2^{63}-1$ (really big numbers). The definition and assignment of `int`, `short` and `long` types are the same, only the size of the numbers they can hold are different (and of course the memory size they will take proportional to the number length they store).

❖ Another integer variable type is `byte`. A byte can store numbers between –128 to 127. In computers, a byte represents 8 bits (binary digits). 8 bits can have the values between 8 zeros (00000000) to 8 ones (11111111). There are 256 numbers in between these numbers therefore they are mapped to -128 to 127 range which contain 256 numbers. In the following code we define a `byte` variable `a` and print it on the terminal:

```
package com.example.atomic.javabasics1;
public class JavaBasics3 {
    public static void main(String args[]) {
        byte a = 100;
        System.out.println(a);
    }
}
```
Code 4.9

If we try to assign a number which is not in the range of −128 and 127 to a `byte`, the compiler gives an error as shown in Figure 4.12.

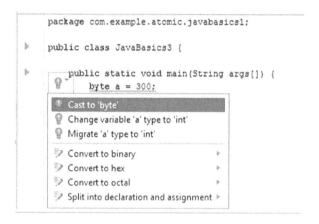

Figure 4.12. Java compiler error

In this figure, the type of the variable `a` is byte therefore it cannot accommodate the value of 300. When we write an incorrect statement, Java compiler gives an error by underlining the errorneous code with red line and shows a red bulb at the incorrect line(s). If we click on these red bulbs, the compiler gives recommendations for correcting our expression.

❖ The last but not the least important integer variable type is `char`. It stores value between 0 and 65535 which constitutes 16 bits (= 2 bytes). `char` type is generally used to hold characters. We can think the characters to be a single letter, a single number or a single symbol like those on our keyboard. In computers, characters are usually mapped to integers via the American Standard Code for Information Interchange (ASCII) table which can be viewed at http://www.asciitable.com. The `char` types in Java use Unicode system which is a superset of ASCII. As an example, the character d is assigned to the variable `myChar` which is of the `char` type variable in the following code:

```
package com.example.atomic.javabasics1;
public class JavaBasics3 {
    public static void main(String args[]) {
        char myChar = 'd';
        System.out.println(a);
    }
}
```
Code 4.10

Please note that the characters assigned to `char` variables are written inside single quotes to tell the Java compiler that this value is of character type. The terminal output of this code is shown below:

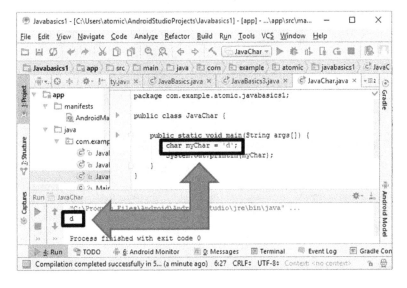

Figure 4.13. `char` definition in Java

3. Decimal variables: Integer variables can only be used to store whole numbers that don't have a fractional part. Decimals (numbers with fractional parts) are represented by two types in Java: `float` and `double`. Their difference is the number of the fractional digits they can hold. `float` types can store 7 fractional digits while this number is 16 for `double` types. Two variables are defined in the following code snippet with **double** and `float` types and then they are printed to see what Java can get from their initializations:

```
package com.helloworld.quantum.helloworld;
public class JavaBasics2 {
    public static void main(String args[]){
        float myFloat = 1.12345678901234567890f;
        double myDouble = 1.12345678901234567890;
        System.out.println("myFloat is: " + myFloat
+ ", myDouble is: " + myDouble);
    }
}
```
Code 4.11

Please note that, the decimal number trying to be assigned to `myFloat` variable is written by an `f` letter at the end in the above code (`1.12345678901234567890f`). This is because Java tries to take any compiler that we want to create a `float` type variable. The output of this code in Android Studio is shown below:

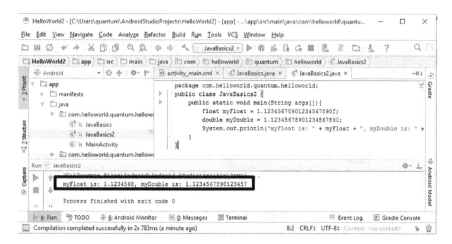

Figure 4.14. `float` and `double` types in Java

In Code 4.10, we tried to assign the number 1.12345678901234567890 to both `myFloat` and `myDouble` variables. However, as it can be seen from the terminal output of Figure 4.12, Java assigned only 7 fractional digits of this number to `myFloat` while it assigned 16 fractional digits to `myDouble`. Therefore we can see that `float` and `double` types can hold 7 and 16 fractional digits, respectively. It can be argued that `double` type variables are better than `float` type variables because they can hold more digits. However, on the other hand `double` variables take more space in the memory. Hence, if memory is not a concern in our Java or Android applications, we can use `double` for better precision whereas it is better to use `float` where memory is a problem.

We have learned **primitive types** until here which are built into Java language and store actual values. The second main class of variables are **reference types**. Reference types do not store values; instead they store addresses of the **objects** they refer. So what is an object? An object is a conceptual bundle that consists of values and related methods (operations that can be applied on values).

There are several forms of reference types. The two widely used types are arrays and classes. Arrays are variable types that store multiple values of the same type in an ordered fashion. A typical array can be illustrated as in Table 4.1.

Index	Value
0	'J'
1	'a'
2	'v'
3	'a'

Table 4.1. Structure of an array

Arrays have indices and values. The values of the array shown above are of `char` type however the value can be of any primitive or reference type as long as all values are of the same type.

Array elements have indices for accessing, deleting them or changing their entries. Indices of arrays always start with 0 and increase one by one. We can use the following code for defining the array shown above:

```
char[] myArray = {'J','a','v','a'};
```
Code 4.12

We can access each element of this array using the following form: `myArray[index]`. We can print the first and the second elements of this array in the terminal as shown in Figure 4.15.

Figure 4.15. Printing elements of a `char` array

The elements of arrays can be changed separately as follows:

```
myArray[1] = 'v';
```
Code 4.13

The second element of `myArray` is changed from 'a' to 'v' by this code. After this line, the contents of the array are: ['J', 'v', 'v', 'a'].

In Java, elements of arrays cannot be deleted because the size of an array is fixed when it is created. We cannot also append new element to arrays for the same reason.

Arrays are useful while dealing with series of data of the same type. For example, if we want to save the data gathered from the acceleration sensor, we can use an array having `float` or `double` type elements.

Another widely used reference type in Java is the `String`. Strings store multiple characters. The first letter of `String` is capitalized because `Strings` are in fact objects in Java. The following code creates a `String` and initializes it to "Let's have a pizza". Please note that values of `Strings` are written in double quotes:

```
String name = "Let's have a pizza";
```
Code 4.14

Since `Strings` are objects, they have related methods for operation on their values. For example, the method `.length()` returns the number of characters in a string as shown below:

```
int stringLength = name.length();
```
Code 4.15

In this code, the length of the `String` named "name" is obtained by `name.length()` and then assigned to a newly created integer variable `stringLength`. The result of this operation in Android Studio is shown in the following figure:

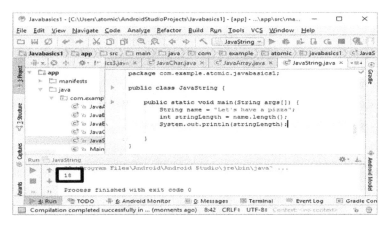

Figure 4.16. Basic `String` operations in Java

BEGINNER'S GUIDE TO ANDROID APP DEVELOPMENT

Java output shows that the `String` "Let's have a pizza" has 18 characters. It is because the spaces in a `String` are also counted as separate characters.

There are dozens of other methods those can be applied on Strings. We'll utilize them when we develop complete Android apps in the next chapters.

Developers sometimes need variables that do not vary ☺. I mean variables whose values cannot be changed after it is initialized. These are called **constants** in programming languages. Java does not a specific keyword for defining a constant but using the keyword `final` in front of a variable declaration makes it a constant as follows:

```
final double pi = 3.1415926535897932384626;
```
Code 4.16

In this code, the `final` keyword makes the variable `pi` immutable (unchangeable) making it effectively a constant. If we try to change a constant, the compiler issues an error as shown in the following figure:

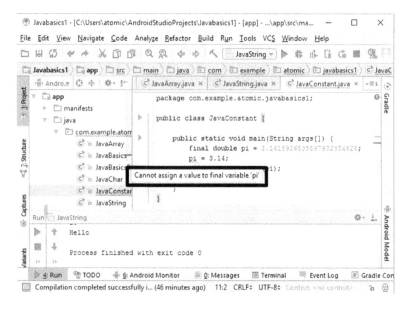

Figure 4.17. Compiler error when a constant is tried to be changed

Our next subsection is about the logical decision making structures in Java, let's have a coffee break and then continue with if-else and switch-case statements.

4.4. Logical Decision Making Statements in Java

Decision making is a widely in programming as in daily life problems. We frequently make logical decisions in daily life such as:

- "**If** their coffee is tasty I'll get another one, **else** I'll grab a tea".

- "**If** it's rainy I'll take my umbrella, **else** I'll not".

In a programming language, decision making statements controls if a condition is met or not as in real life. There are two decision making statements in Java: **if–else** and **switch–case** blocks.

If–else structure: In this conditional, if the condition is satisfied, the code inside the **if block** is executed. If the condition isn't satisfied, then the code in the **else block** is executed. Hence, if we need tell the rainy – not rainy example using an if–else block, we do it as follows:

if it's rainy {

      I'll take my umbrella.

}

else {

      I'll not take my umbrella.

}

Let's see how we can check if two numbers are equal in Java using an if-else statement:

```
package com.helloworld.quantum.helloworld;
public class JavaIfElse {
    public static void main(String args[]){
        int a = 4;
        int b = 4;
        if (a == b){
```

```
        System.out.println("a and b are equal");
            }
  else   {
        System.out.println("a and b are not equal");
            }
        }
}
```

Code 4.17 (cont'd from the previous page)

Let's analyse this code:

➢ In this code, two integer type variables, `a` and `b`, are created and initialized to 4.
➢ In the next line, the `if` statement checks if `a` and `b` are equal.
➢ The comparison operator `==` is used to check the equality.
➢ If the result of this comparison is true, the statement inside the if block `System.out.println("a and b are equal");` is executed which prints "a and b are equal" on the terminal screen.
➢ If the result of this comparison is false, the statement inside the if block `System.out.println("a and b are not equal");` is executed which prints "a and b are not equal" on the terminal screen.

Since we initialized both `a` and `b` to 4, they are equal and the Java compiler executes the code inside the `if` block as follows:

Figure 4.18. if –else example in Java

When we change one of the numbers to something other than 4, the code inside the `else` block is executed as shown in Figure 4.19.

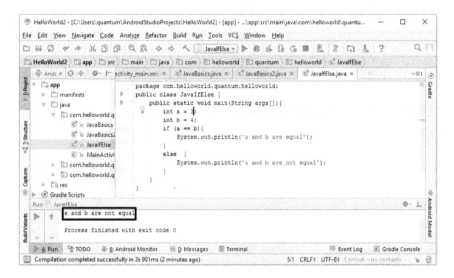

Figure 4.19. if–else statement in Java when the condition not satisfied

If–else statements can also be used in nested forms as in Code 4.17. In nested statements, the conditions are checked from top to down. When a condition is satisfied, then the code inside its block is executed and the program ends. If none of the conditions are true, then the final `else` block is executed. **In other words, the statements in the last else block is executed if none of the conditions above it are satisfied.** The screenshot of this nested code in the playground is given in Figure 4.20.

```
package com.helloworld.quantum.helloworld;
public class JavaNestedIfElse {
    public static void main(String args[]){
        int a = 3;
        int b = 4;
        if (a == b){
          System.out.println("a and b are equal");
        }
        else if(a > b) {
          System.out.println("a is greater than b");
        }
        else {
          System.out.println("a is lower than b");
        }
```

```
        }
    }
```

Code 4.18 (cont'd from the previous page)

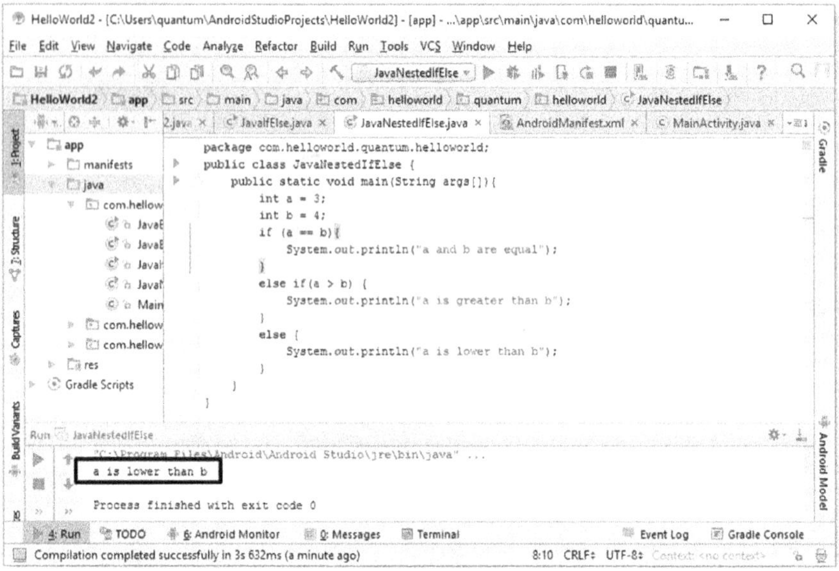

Figure 4.20. Nested if–else statements in Java

Nested if–else decision making statements become error-prone as more and more conditions are added. In order to check a lot of conditions easier, **switch–case** statements are used. Switch–case statements work similar to nested if–else statements but they are easier for checking multiple conditions. A switch–case statement for assessing the grade of a student is shown in Code 4.18.

```
package com.helloworld.quantum.helloworld;
public class JavaSwitchCase {
    public static void main(String args[]){
        char grade = 'B';
        switch (grade) {
            case 'A':
    System.out.println("Your grade is excellent.");
                break;
            case 'B':
    System.out.println("Your grade is very good.");
                break;
            case 'C':
```

```
        System.out.println("Your grade is good.");
                break;
            case 'D':
        System.out.println("Your grade is low. You have
to take the course again.");
                break;
            case 'E':
        System.out.println("Your grade is very low. You
have to take the course again.");
                break;
            default:
        System.out.println("Not a valid grade");

        }
    }
}
```

Code 4.19 (cont'd from the previous page)

In this example, the grade variable has the type **char**. This variable is switched and checked against the characters 'A', 'B', 'C', 'D', 'E'. The switched variable is initialized to 'B' therefore the code block inside the **case 'B' :** will be executed. It is worth noting the **break;** statements in each case block; **break** makes the whole switch block to end as it is needed in this example. Please note the **default:** block at the end of the program. The code block inside **default** is executed when none of the above cases are satisfied. If we enter a character other than 'A', 'B', 'C', 'D' and 'E', the program will print "Not a valid grade" on the terminal. A **default** block is not mandatory in Java but useful as we'll see in Android app development chapters.

Selecting if–else or switch–case: If the checked variable has a lot of discrete values, switch–case blocks are easier to use.

We'll use decision making statements a lot in Android app development. Let's now study another widely used concept: loops.

4.5. Loops in Java

Performing an operation in a repeated form is frequently needed in programming. These repetitions are performed using loops. Programming would be very difficult and long without loops. For example, let's try to find the sum of numbers from 1 to 50. Without loops, what we would do is as follows:

```
int sum = 0
sum = sum + 1
sum = sum + 2
sum = sum + 3
.... (44 more lines of code here)
sum = sum + 48
sum = sum + 49
sum = sum + 50
```
Code 4.20

There has to be 44 more lines of code in the line shown by dots (shortened above). As you can see, this simple task would require 51 lines of code without loops. Moreover, it's error prone. Please remember that we want to perform things in programming with shortest code possible to prevent errors.

There are three types of loops in Java: `for` loop, `while` loop and `do-while` loop.

1. `for` loop: We use `for` loops when we know how many times an operation will be performed. The general structure of a `for` loop is as follows:

```
for (type counter = initial value; counter check;
counter increment/decrement statement) {
    Code to be performed repeatedly
  }
```
Code 4.21

➢ The `counter` is an integer variable.
➢ The `counter` variable is incremented or decremented according to the expression in (`counter increment/decrement statement`) after each cycle.
➢ After each increment/decrement, the `counter` is checked if the (`counter check`) is still satisfied. If it is satisfied, the loop continues; if not satisfied, the loop ends.

Let's calculate the sum of numbers from 1 to 50 using a `for` loop to understand these better:

```
package com.helloworld.quantum.helloworld;
public class JavaFor {
    public static void main(String args[]){
  int sum = 0;
  for (int counter = 0; counter <=50; counter++){
    sum = sum + counter;
  }
  System.out.println("Sum is " + sum);
  }
}
```
Code 4.22

In this code, a variable called `sum` is created to hold the sum. Then, a `for` loop is defined in which an integer variable named `counter` is created and looped from 0 to 50. In the `for` loop, the loop variable counter is incremeneted by 1 in each iteration by the expression `counter++`. Therefore, the `counter` variable takes the values of 0, 1, 2, 3, ..., 50 as the loop continues to cycle. When it takes the value 51, the loop condition `counter=<50`, which means equal or lower than 50, is not satisfied therefore the loop ends without performing the loop operation for `counter = 51`.

The variable `sum` is initialized to 0 and then the `counter` is added to it in the loop block by the expression: `sum=sum+counter`. This method adds the numbers from 0 to 50 to the `sum` variable. In the end, the `sum` variable is printed on the terminal screen as in Figure 4.21. The sum of the numbers from 0 to 50 is calculated as 1275.

2. `while` loop: while loops can be used even when we don't know at which iteration the cycle will end. The main difference of `for` and `while` loops is that the incrementing method of the loop variable is specified inside the loop therefore it provides a bit more flexibility. The calculation of the sum of numbers from 0 to 50 using a `while` loop is shown in Code 4.23.

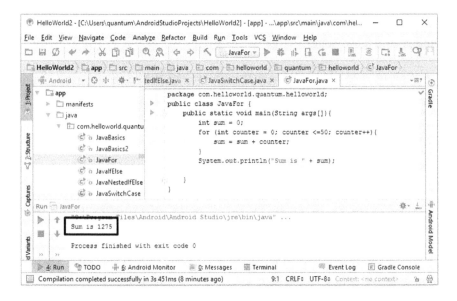

Figure 4.21. `for` loop example in Java

```
package com.helloworld.quantum.helloworld;
public class JavaWhile {
    public static void main(String args[]){
        int sum = 0;
        int counter = 0;
        while (counter <=50){
            sum = sum + counter;
            counter++;
        }
        System.out.println("Sum is " + sum);
    }
}
```
Code 4.23

As you can see from above, the loop variable `counter` is defined before the `while` loop. The `while` loop checks if the condition `counter=<50` is satisfied. When it is satisfied, the expressions inside the `while` loop are executed, otherwise the loop ends. The `counter` variable is incremented inside the `while` loop by the expression `counter++`. The output is again 1275 as shown in Figure 4.22.

Figure 4.22. `while` loop example in Java

3. `do-while` loop: `do-while` performs similar to the `while` loop except the loop variable is checked at the end of the loop block as follows:

```java
package com.example.atomic.javabasics1;
public class JavaDoWhile {
    public static void main(String args[]) {
        int sum = 0;
        int counter = 0;
        do {
            sum = sum + counter;
            counter++;
        }while (counter<=50);
        // do-while loop ends here
        System.out.println("The sum is " + sum);
    }
}
```
Code 4.24

The sum is again calculated as 1275 in this code. As we can see from above code, `while` and `do-while` are very similar. On the other hand, please note the code `//do-while loop ends here`. This is a

73

comment line in Java. The compiler ignores anything written next to //.
Comments are used for increasing the readability of the code.

The output of the `do-while` program is shown below:

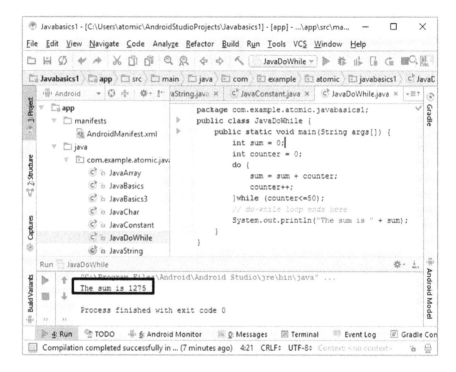

Figure 4.23. `do-while` loop example in Java

Note: There are two important keywords that are used to further control
loops: `break` and `continue` statements.

These commands are usually used together with an `if` statement. The
`break` command breaks the loop; it means the program quits the current
loop before the loop condition expires. On the other hand, `continue`
command makes the loop continue with the next iteration

4.6. Methods in Java

Methods are subroutines that are used for performing an operation.
Methods are similar to functions in other programming languages but the
difference is that methods are always associated with classes and objects.

Because of this, methods are always defined inside classes. The general form of a function is as in Code 4.24.

```
(public)     (void)      (return     type)     methodName
(arguments) {
........ (code inside the method)
(return output_values;)
}
```
Code 4.25

A method declaration has the following parts:

➤ The name of the method (`methodName`).
➤ Method identifiers like `public` and `static` (optional).
➤ Arguments (input values) of the method (optional).
➤ The type of return values (optional).
➤ The `void` keyword–used if the method won't output any value (optional).
➤ `return` keyword for outputting return values (optional).
➤ The statements that will perform the operatioṅ.

Let's write a method that adds two integers and prints the sum on the terminal:

```
static void addNumbers(int a, int b) {
    int sum;
    sum = a + b;
    System.out.println("The sum is " + sum);
}
```
Code 4.26

In this method:

➤ The `static` keyword is used that means this method can be called without creating an object of its class.
➤ `void` keyword is used because the method won't output any values; it will just print on the terminal screen.
➤ Inputs (arguments) of the method has two input variables `a` and `b` which both are of the `int` type.

➢ The sum is calculated inside the function and assigned to the **sum** variable. Please note that the variables which are defined inside the function cannot be accessed outside the function.
➢ Finally, the sum is printed on the terminal screen with the usual **System.out.println()** method.

When we define a method, it doesn't run automatically. We need to call it with its input arguments. We do this by writing its name and arguments as follows:

```
addNumbers(2, 5);
```
Code 4.27

When we call this method, the input arguments are 2 and 5. The method will add these numbers and print the result on the screen. The complete code of the method definition and its call is as follows:

```
package com.example.atomic.javabasics1;
public class JavaMethodAdd1 {

    public static void main(String args[]){
        addNumbers(2, 5);
    }
    static void addNumbers(int a, int b){
        int sum;
        sum = a + b;
        System.out.println("The sum is " + sum);
    }
}
```
Code 4.28

When we run this program in Android Studio, we get the terminal output shown in Figure 4.24.

This function didn't have return values. Let's modify it so that the sum of the input values will be given as a return value. We can do this modification by just adding the following line instead of the **System.out.println()**:

```
return sum;
```
Code 4.29

We also have to replace the `void` keyword to `int` keyword as shown in Code 4.29 because the function will output an `int` type variable (`sum`).

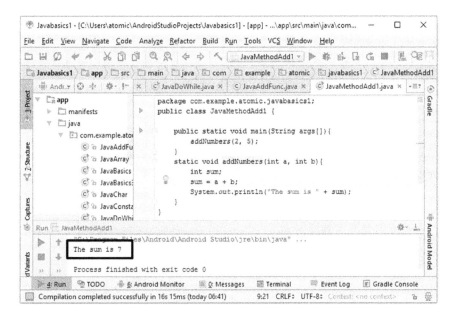

Figure 4.24. Method definition and calling in Java

```
package com.example.atomic.javabasics1;
public class JavaMethodAdd2 {

    public static void main(String args[]){
        addNumbers(2, 5);
    }
    static int addNumbers(int a, int b){
        int sum;
        sum = a + b;
        return sum;
    }
}
```
Code 4.30

When we run the code above, nothing happens because we removed the printing code from the method and it only outputs the sum. We can print the output of the method as follows:

```
package com.example.atomic.javabasics1;
public class JavaMethodAdd2 {
```

```
public static void main(String args[]){
    System.out.println(addNumbers(2, 5));
}
static int addNumbers(int a, int b){
    int sum;
    sum = a + b;
    return sum;
}
}
```

Code 4.31 (cont'd from the previous page)

We have written the method call inside the `System.out.println()` method therefore the return value of the method will be printed as shown below:

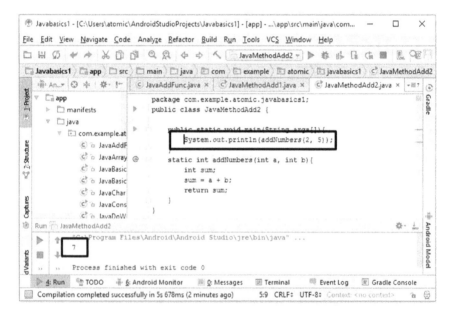

Figure 4.25. Using a method that returns a value

Methods provide us a good way of shortening our code and making it compact as we can see from these simple examples. Of course their usage range is not only simple mathematical operations, a Java or an Android application contains a lot of user defined and ready methods available from the Android SDK or Java SDK. Android SDK includes thousands of methods which makes the developers' lives easier.

Methods are also important to share code among developers. If we can find a ready-coded method on the Internet, we can utilize it in our apps easily.

Methods are always parts of classes. So, let's now focus on classes, objects and inheritance that are the backbones of the so-called "object-oriented programming".

4.7. Classes, Objects and Inheritance in Java

Java programming language uses traditional (procedural) and object-oriented concepts together for a stronger experience. Procedural programming means that a program uses procedures and functions executed by order. This is the traditional method. On the other side, object-oriented programming uses classes and objects derived from these classes to execute the required computational steps. So, what are classes and objects?

We can think classes as blueprints and objects as different products made using this blueprint. Similarly, we can consider a car factory as an example for classes and objects. Imagine a car production band. Each time we change the colour, baggage size, steering wheel type, etc., we obtain a different car without changing the basic properties of the car. If the car make and model are Virtuma and Liberty (hypothetical names!), the production band produces Virtuma Liberty 1.6, Virtuma Liberty 2.0, Virtuma Liberty 3.0, Virtuma Liberty 1.6 premium, Virtuma Liberty 2.0 diesel, etc. In this case the class is Virtuma Liberty and all these hypothetical models are objects belonging to this class. We can imagine this as in Figure 4.26.

Let's declare a `Car` class in Java first and then define different car objects derived from this class as in Code 4.31. In this code, a class named `Car` is defined by `public static class Car` which has variables named `colour`, `fuel_type` and `engine_capacity`. These are the variables which will be different for each object derived from this class.

Inside the class definition, there is a method declaration `public Car(String carColour, String carFuelType, float`

79

`CarEngineCapacity)`. This is a constructor method having the same name with the class name and the class variables are assigned inside this method by the code lines shown in Code 4.33.

Class   Objects

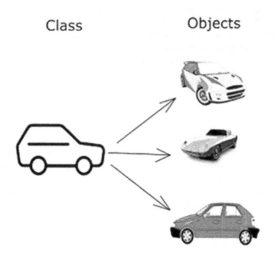

Figure 4.26. Class–object relationship by example

```
package com.helloworld.quantum.helloworld;
public class JavaClassMain1 {
    public static class Car {
        static String colour;
        static String fuel_type;
        static float engine_capacity;
        public Car(String carColour, String
carFuelType, float CarEngineCapacity){
            colour=carColour;
            fuel_type=carFuelType;
            engine_capacity = CarEngineCapacity;
    }
    }

    public static void main(String args[]){
        Car myCar = new Car("Red", "Diesel", 1.2f);
        System.out.println(myCar.colour);
    }
}
```
Code 4.32

```
colour=carColour;
fuel_type=carFuelType;
engine_capacity = CarEngineCapacity;
```
Code 4.33

Finally, inside the main function of the program, a `Car` object called `myCar` is created with the line:

```
Car myCar = new Car("Red", "Diesel", 1.2f);
```
Code 4.34

Please note that the `new` keyword is used for creating an object using a class. We can read this object declaration line as "An object named `myCar` is created using the `Car` class with the parameters of "`Red`", "`Diesel`" and "`1.2f`" ".

Once the object is created, we access its variables and methods using a dot operator (.). In the last code line of Code 4.31, the colour variable of `myCar` object is extracted by the expression `myCar.colour` and then printed on the terminal. The output is the colour variable of the myCar object as shown in Figure 4.27.

We can define any number of different objects using our class like:

```
Car yourCar = new Car("White", "Gasoline", 1.6f);
Car newCar = new Car("Grey", "Diesel", 2.0f);
```
Code 4.5

The power of class–object concept stems from the availability of both variables and methods from a single object and the possibility of using the same class structure for various object definitions easily.

We can add a method to the class with the usual method definition. For example, let's add a method to display the fuel type as shown in Code 4.35.

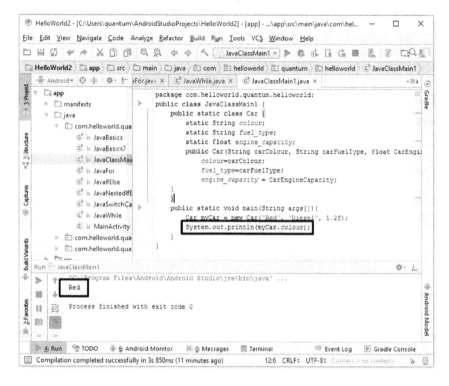

Figure 4.27. Class and object example in Java

```
package com.helloworld.quantum.helloworld;
public class JavaClassMain1 {
    public static class Car {
        static String colour;
        static String fuel_type;
        static float engine_capacity;
        public Car(String carColour, String
carFuelType, float CarEngineCapacity){
            colour=carColour;
            fuel_type=carFuelType;
            engine_capacity = CarEngineCapacity;
    }
        public void askFuelType(){
            System.out.println(fuel_type);
        }
    }
    public static void main(String args[]){
        Car myCar = new Car("Red", "Diesel", 1.2f);
        myCar.askFuelType();
    }
```

```
}
```
Code 4.36 (cont'd from the previous page)

In this modified code, a method called `askFuelType` is added to the `Car` class definition that prints the `fuel_type` variable on the terminal. In the main method, the newly added method is called again by the dot operator (`.`):

```
myCar.askFuelType();
```
Code 4.37

Please note that methods without arguments are called by empty parentheses `()`. The `askFuelType` method is called and it does its duty as shown below:

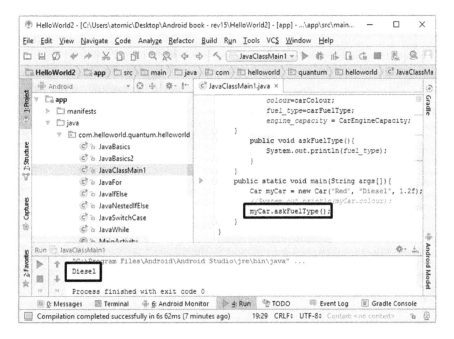

Figure 4.28. Calling a method of a class in Java

The basic class and object relation can be summarized as in the above code samples. However, there's another important property of classes which is another advantage of object-oriented programming: inheritance. Inheritance is basically the ability of creating an extended new class (let's call this as class$_2$) from an existing class (class$_1$). The child class

83

(class$_2$) will have the fields and methods of its parent class (class$_1$). The child class may also have new variables and methods too.

We have defined a `Car` class in Code 4.36. Let's define a child class called `sedanCar` that will extend the parent class `Car`:

```
public static class sedanCar extends Car{
  int b_Vol;
  public sedanCar(String carColour, String
    carFuelType, float CarEngineCapacity, int
    baggageVol) {
      super(carColour, carFuelType,
        CarEngineCapacity);
    b_Vol = baggageVol;
    }
}
```
Code 4.38

In the first line of this code, the new (child) class `sedanCar` **extends** the `Car` class. Then, a new integer type variable `b_Vol` is declared in the new class. Next, a constructor method for the `sedanCar` is defined by `public sedanCar(String carColour, String carFuelType, float CarEngineCapacity, int baggageVol)`. Inside this constructor, there is an important code line:

```
super(carColour, carFuelType, CarEngineCapacity);
```
Code 4.39

In Java, the `super` keyword is used to invoke the constructors of the parent class in a child class. Therefore, the child class `sedanCar` inherits the fields (variables for this case) of the parent class using the `super` keyword.

The complete code of parent and child classes is given in Code 4.40.

```
package com.helloworld.quantum.helloworld;
public class JavaClassMain1 {
    public static class Car {
        static String colour;
        static String fuel_type;
        static float engine_capacity;
        public Car(String carColour, String
carFuelType, float CarEngineCapacity){
```

```
            colour=carColour;
            fuel_type=carFuelType;
            engine_capacity = CarEngineCapacity;
    }
        public void askFuelType(){
            System.out.println(fuel_type);
        }
    }

    public static class sedanCar extends Car{
        int b_Vol;
        public sedanCar(String carColour, String
          carFuelType, float CarEngineCapacity,
          int baggageVol) {
            super(carColour, carFuelType,
              CarEngineCapacity);
            b_Vol = baggageVol;
        }

    }

    public static void main(String args[]){
        sedanCar newCar = new sedanCar("Red",
                          "Diesel", 1.2f, 40);
        newCar.askFuelType();
        System.out.println(newCar.b_Vol);
    }
}
```

Code 4.40 (cont'd from the previous page)

We can apply the method askFuelType on the object newCar derived from the child class despite the child class doesn't have askFuelType method explicitly. This is because the child class inherits all methods of its parent class therefore sedanCar class actually has the askFuelType method.

In the last line, the b_Vol variable that is unique to the child class is accessed as usual. The output of this code in Android Studio is shown in Figure 4.29.

If the classes and objects make you confused, don't worry. You'll understand them better when we use them for developing Android apps.

Java is, of course, a very extensive programming language and Java SDK has thousands of methods for developing sophisticated Java programs. However, I think this much of Java basics lecture is enough for starting to develop Android apps. I'm sure you'll get used to writing Java code in the upcoming chapters.

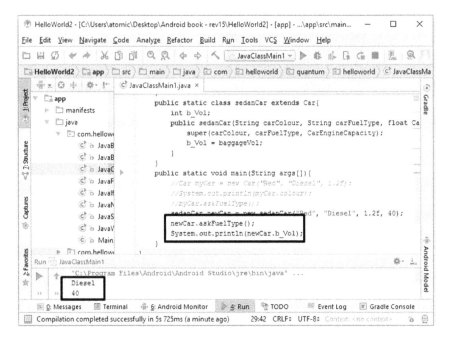

Figure 4.29. Class extension example in Java

The good news is that the boring stuff ends here and the fun is beginning: actual Android app development–developing apps that actually do something. We'll design apps that interact with the user and use the wonders of Android platform such as SMS sending and GPS reading. Let's have a coffee and relax for some time before beginning the next chapter where we'll start our Android app development journey.

ANDRIOD APP #1: RED/BLUE LIGHTHEAD

We'll develop a simple strobe light app in this project. We'll go through accessing the button in Java code, getting the screen background colour, setting this colour and sensing button taps to change the background colour.

Our aim is to develop an Android app where the background colour of the app is varied as in a red/blue strobe light. The background colour of the app will change from red to blue or vice versa each time we click a button located in the middle of the screen. This is a very simple app but will teach the basics steps of visual programming.

5.1. Creating a New Android Project

Firstly, please select "Create a new project". If Android Studio is already running select File → New → New Project from the top menu as shown below:

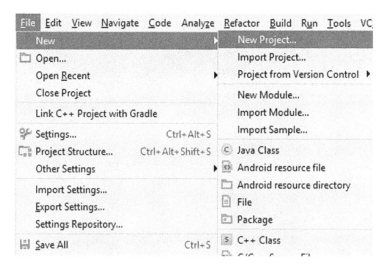

Figure 5.1. Creating a new project in Android Studio

I named the app as "Lighthead app" as shown in Figure 5.2, but you can give any name you'd like to.

Figure 5.2. Naming the app

Then, I selected the app to be compatible with phones and tablets having Android 4.0.3 (Ice Cream Sandwich) or later:

Figure 5.3. Selecting app compatibility

We'll have a simple screen therefore "Empty Activity" does the job in the next dialog:

Figure 5.4. Selecting the screen layout

Finally, leave the name of the activity as "MainActivity" and then click "Finish" to create the project files:

Figure 5.5. Final settings

After the project is successfully created, the default view of the Android Studio will appear in which the middle pane will show the "MainActivity.java" file as shown below:

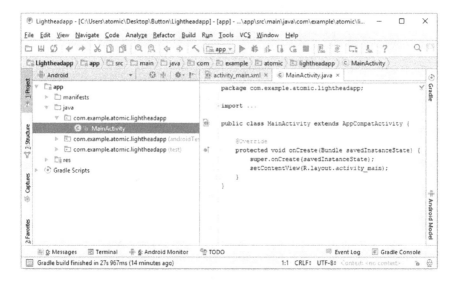

Figure 5.6. Default view in Android Studio

5.2. Developing the User Interface

Let's open the user interface layout file **activity_main.xml** where we will place the button on the screen. As we can see from the figure above, the left pane shows the folders and files of our project. Make sure that the view type is **Android** and select the folders **res → layout** and then double-click on the file **activity_main.xml** there as shown in Figure 5.7.

When the **activity_main.xml** file is opened, the layout it contains will be shown in the middle pane as shown in Figure 5.8. This file and other xml files contain the layout information of an Android app in Android Studio. In fact, **xml** files are not only used in Android app development but also in other areas of computing. **xml** files are good to express the relations among different entities in a hierarchical way therefore is a good choice to use in layout design. **xml** files are text files but Android Studio interprets them as layouts as long as they are in the correct format. We can also view the text file representation of **activity_main.xml** in

Android Studio by selecting the **Text** tab as indicated by the arrow in Figure 5.8.

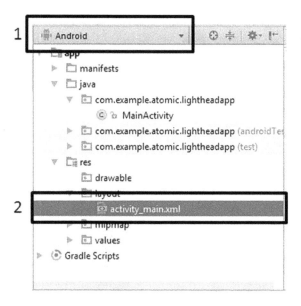

Figure 5.7. Finding activity_main.xml file in project explorer

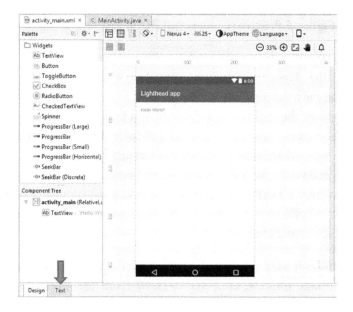

Figure 5.8. Viewing **activity_main** in Android Studio

When the Text tab is selected, the text format of the activity_main.xml file is displayed in the middle pane as follows:

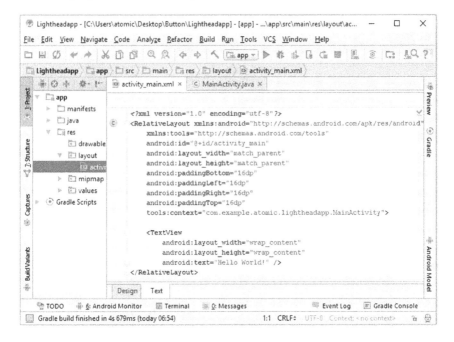

Figure 5.9. activity_main.xml file in text representation

You don't need to be confused about the contents of this file. We'll do most of the layout operations visually. We'll only use this text representation in special cases. However, it is a good practice to follow the contents of the xml file as we design app layouts. In the above figure, we can see that our layout consists of a **RelativeLayout** structure, which begins by the line **<RelativeLayout...** and ends with **</RelativeLayout>**. Inside this layout, we have a **TextView** component. In other words, a **TextView** component exists inside the **RelativeLayout** component. Let's now see how an Android app GUI is built in general using these components.

In Android, all user graphical user interface (GUI) objects (widgets, layouts, image objects, etc.) are derived from the View class of the GUI library. The basic hierarchy of GUI classes are shown in Figure 5.10.

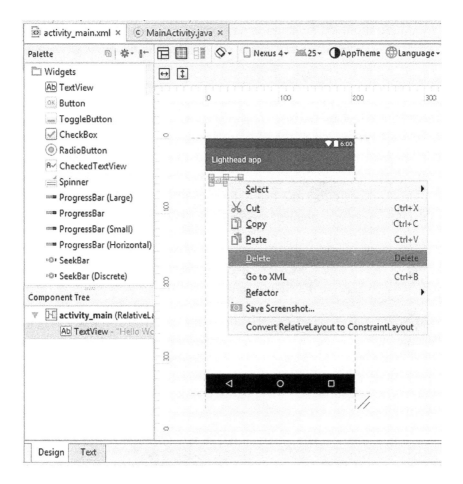

Figure 5.10. Basic hierarchy of the GUI components

The components of the GUI of an Android app have the following basic properties:

➢ Because all GUI objects are derived from the **View** class, these GUI objects are also called as **view**s in Android programming.

➢ **ViewGroup**'s child classes **RelativeLayout**, **LinearLayout**, **AbsoluteLayout** and **GridLayout** are special views that can contain other views and components. These are used for shaping the layout as you wish.

➢ An Android GUI should consist of at least one layout class. For example, our `activity_main.xml` file has the `RelativeLayout` as shown in Figure 5.9.

➢ We can build any GUI by using the subclasses of the `View` class shown in Figure 5.10.

We'll see several GUI designs during our app development journey. Different developers prefer different strategies for shaping their app's GUI. In my personal opinion, RelativeLayout provides more flexibility therefore easier to use. The basic property of the RelativeLayout is that each GUI object is positioned relative to each other.

Anyway, let's continue developing our red/blue strobe light app. Please switch to the **Design** view of the **activity_main.xml** file as in Figure 5.8 so that we can design the GUI visually.

First of all, please delete the default "Hello World" TextView by right-clicking on it and selecting "Delete" as shown below:

Figure 5.11. Deleting the default "Hello World" TextView

After deleting the default TextView, please find the **Button** widget from the objects palette and then drag and drop it in the middle of the GUI by the help of the guiding lines as shown in Figure 5.12.

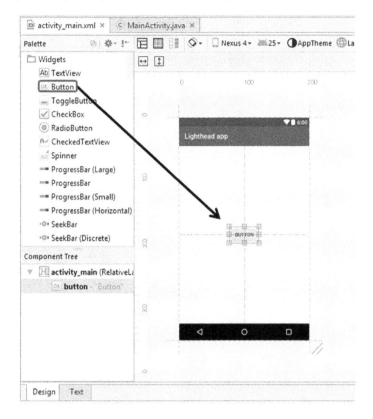

Figure 5.12. Adding a button widget in the middle of the user interface

When we add a widget to the GUI, it keeps being selected and then its properties can be viewed from the right pane as shown in Figure 5.13. The basic properties of the button are shown in this pane. However, we can see the full list of properties by clicking on the **View all properties** (can be seen after scrolling down) as shown in Figure 5.14.

Anyway, let's go on with the basic properties pane shown inside the rectangle in Figure 5.13. In this pane, one of the most important properties for accessing the button is the ID. All objects of the GUI of an Android app are accessed through their IDs in the coding part.

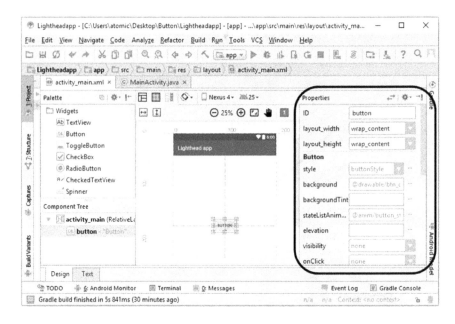

Figure 5.13. Basic properties of the button widget

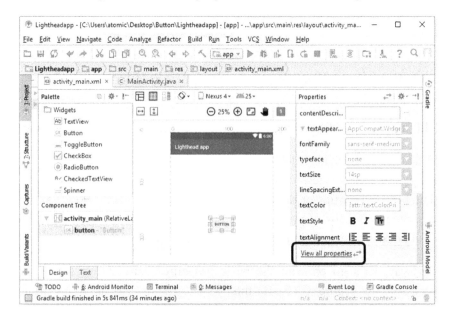

Figure 5.14. Switching to all properties of the button widget

In our app, the default ID of the button widget is set as **button** by Android Studio. We can change it just by clicking the ID box and replacing the **button** text.

The next two boxes refer to the **layout width** and **layout height** properties of the button widget. Their settings determine the width and the height of the button object in the GUI. They are set as **wrap_content** by default. This means that the width and the height of the button will be adjusted to wrap (cover) the text written inside the button (i.e. button's label). The other available choice for these parameters is the **match_parent** as shown in Figure 5.15. If this is selected, the respective property (width or height) will be equal to the width or height of its parent container (which is the RelativeLayout covering the whole screen in this example).

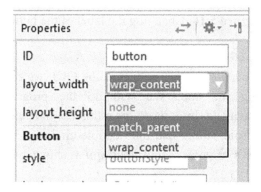

Figure 5.15. The alternatives for the layout_width and layout_height parameters

Since we don't want the button to have a width or height filling the whole GUI, we need to leave these parameters having the value of **wrap_content**.

In our app, the button is supposed to change the background colour of the screen therefore it is good to change the label of the button accordingly. The button's label (the text on the button) is **Button** by default. Let's change it to "Change!" as shown in Figure 5.16.

Figure 5.16. Changing the label of the button

5.3. Writing the Main Code of the App

Since we don't need any other widget in the GUI, we can now continue to programming the app. We will do the programming in the **MainActivity.java** file. In order to open this file, navigate to the project explorer in Android Studio and then double-click on the **MainActivity** located under **java → com…..lightheadapp** as shown below:

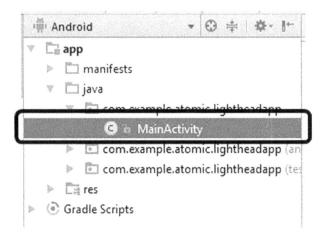

Figure 5.17. Opening the MainActivity.java file in Android Studio

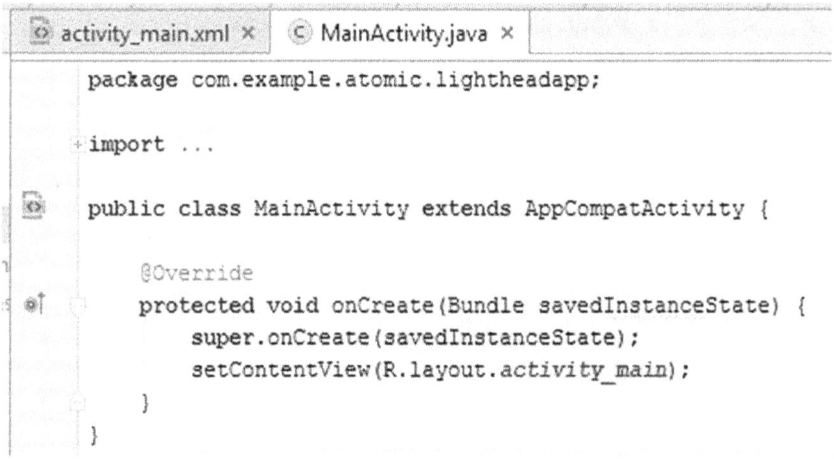

```
activity_main.xml ×    ⓒ MainActivity.java ×

    package com.example.atomic.lightheadapp;

  import ...

    public class MainActivity extends AppCompatActivity {

        @Override
        protected void onCreate(Bundle savedInstanceState) {
            super.onCreate(savedInstanceState);
            setContentView(R.layout.activity_main);
        }
    }
```

Figure 5.18. The default MainActivity.java file

The MainActivity.java file shown above is the default file generated by Android Studio. Some code lines are hidden by default as shown by ... in the `import` line. You can open these codes by clicking on the ... there as shown below:

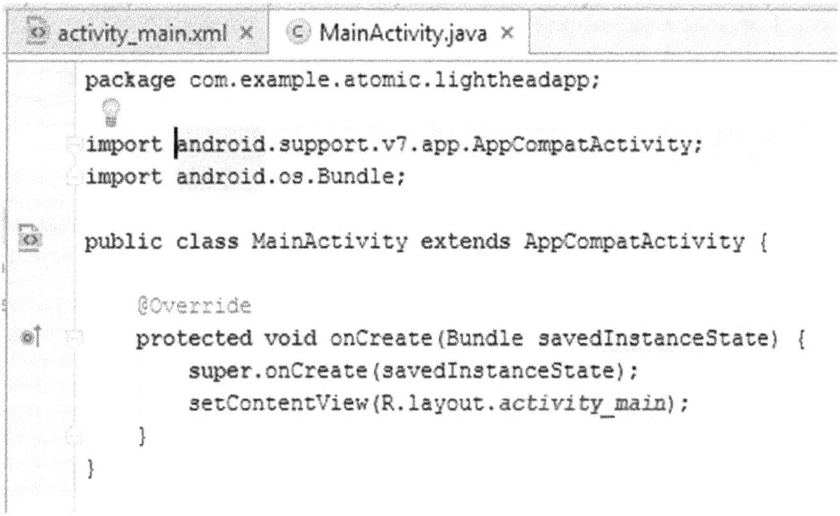

```
activity_main.xml ×    ⓒ MainActivity.java ×

    package com.example.atomic.lightheadapp;

  import android.support.v7.app.AppCompatActivity;
  import android.os.Bundle;

    public class MainActivity extends AppCompatActivity {

        @Override
        protected void onCreate(Bundle savedInstanceState) {
            super.onCreate(savedInstanceState);
            setContentView(R.layout.activity_main);
        }
    }
```

Figure 5.19. The default MainActivity.java file after opening the hidden lines

Let's analyse the default MainActivity.java code line by line:

- ➢ The first line is the `package` definition as in usual Java code. It shows to which package this file belongs to.
- ➢ The next two lines are `import` lines which import the required libraries. In our file, the `AppCompatActivity` and `Bundle` libraries are imported. They contain the base methods for user interaction and passing data among different activities.
- ➢ The next line declares the `MainActivity` class which extends the `AppCompatActivity` class. This is like the class definition in Java. As in Java, the class name in Android should match the name of the .java file. In this case, the file is `MainActivity.java` therefore the name of the class is `MainActivity`.
- ➢ Then an `@override` command is placed by default. It is used to tell the compiler that the current class will override any existing superclasses.
- ➢ The sixth code line defines a method called `onCreate()`. All activities are started by a sequence of method calls. `onCreate()` method is the first of these calls.
- ➢ The next line, `super.onCreate(savedInstanceState);`, tells that our code will be executed in addition to the existing code (if any) of the parent class.
- ➢ In the last line, `setContentView()` method sets the activity content from a layout source. We have set up our app's layout in the file `activity_main.xml`. Android accesses all resources via an auxiliary class called "R". The R class is a special class which enables Android to utilize the resources in a simpler way compared to accessing via file paths. The argument of the `setContentView()` method is `R.layout.activity_main` which means "set the content of the activity to be the layout residing in activity_main.xml".

We hear the word **activity** a lot in Android programming. Activity is a class that manages the user interface and the interaction of the app with the user.

When an activity is launched, it can exist in various states as shown in Figure 5.20.

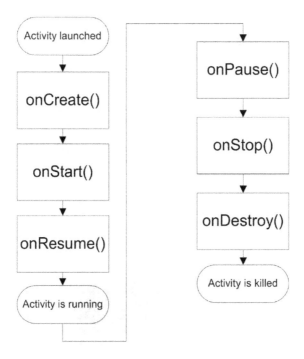

Figure 5.20. Several phases of an activity

As you can see from the figure above, an activity may have several phases. These phases depend on the activity itself as well as the Android operating system. For example, if another activity needs a lot of memory, the current activity may be paused (`onPause()`) because Android gives precedence to the other activity.

In the MainActivity.java file of our app, the `onCreate()` method is called when the activity is first created. All static set up are done inside this method.

If we run our app at this stage, we should see the layout we designed. We can run it in the simulator by hitting the "Run" button and selecting an emulator as we did in Chapter 3. The Nexus 4 emulator running our app is shown in Figure 5.21.

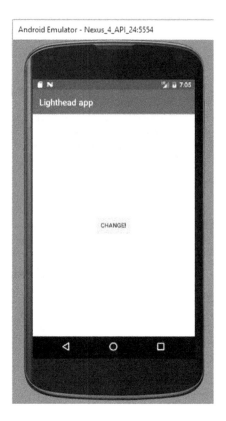

Figure 5.21. The app in the emulator

When we click on the **Change!** button, nothing happens at this stage because we didn't write the code to handle the button clicks yet. Let's code the necessary operations to change background colour by the button clicks as we aim to do for this app.

In order to check the button continuously, the app needs to "listen" the button. Therefore, we need to create a button listener method and call it when the activity first starts. We can give any name to out button listener method such as `myButtonListenerMethod()`. In this method, we need to find the button widget using the mentioned R class and create a button object to access the button. I know this may seem a bit confusing for now but I'm sure you'll get used to it soon. These are shown in Code 5.1.

```
public void myButtonListenerMethod() {
Button button = (Button)
findViewById(R.id.button);
}
```
Code 5.1

We can now access the button using the `button` object that is created by line `Button button=(Button) findViewById(R.id.button)`. `findViewById()` method finds the views (widgets, layouts, etc.) using their IDs. Remember that we have given the ID "button" to our button widget during the layout design. Hence, we accessed it using the `R` class as `R.id.button`.

There is another special method called `setOnClickListener()` in Android SDK. This method continuously listens to the clicks on a button. Everything those will be performed when a click on the button should reside inside this method. This method is applied on the button we want to listen to as follows:

```
public void myButtonListenerMethod() {
button = (Button) findViewById(R.id.button);
button.setOnClickListener(new
View.OnClickListener() {
        @Override
        public void onClick(View v) {
        }
}
```
Code 5.2

In the above code:

➢ A new `onClickListener` is created by `new View.OnClickListener()` and then this object is made an argument to the `setOnClickListener()` method , which is applied on the button object.
➢ It then it overrides the superclass listeners with the `@Override` directive (there's no superclass listeners in our example, this directive is automatically generated by Android Studio).
➢ Finally, a method called `onClick()` is called when the button is clicked.

All code lines that will be run when the button is clicked will go inside the onClick(View v) method.

Note: You'll notice that Android Studio auto-completes your code in an intelligent way. In my opinion, Android Studio is excellent in this feature.

Our aim is to change the background colour from red to blue and vice versa as the button is clicked. In the activity_main.xml file, we saw that our GUI has a RelativeLayout element as the main layout that fills the screen. Because of this, we can access the background using the following code:

```
RelativeLayout    bgElement    =    (RelativeLayout)
findViewById(R.id.activity_main);
```
Code 5.3

In this code, we have generated a RelativeLayout object called bgElement from which we can access all of the properties of the background of the app.

We now need to check the colour of the bgElement. This is because we will change its colour according to its current colour. If it is red now, the button will change it to blue. If it is blue now, the button click will turn it to red.

```
int color = ((ColorDrawable)
bgElement.getBackground()).getColor();
```
Code 5.4

In this code, the colour of the background of the layout of the app is taken by bgElement.getBackground()).getColor(); and then converted to the type ColorDrawable, which expresses the colour as an integer. Then, this integer value is assigned to the color variable. In short, the colour of the background will be expressed in the variable named colour as an integer.

We will now utilize a decision making statement to change the colour such as:

If the colour is red, change to blue; else (= if the colour is blue) change to red.

We can do this by the following code:

```
if (color == Color.RED) {
    bgElement.setBackgroundColor(Color.BLUE);
}
  else {
    bgElement.setBackgroundColor(Color.RED);
}
```
Code 5.5

There's a special class called `Color` in Android SDK for doing colour related operations. The expressions `Color.RED` and `Color.BLUE` represent the integer values corresponding to the red and blue colours, respectively. Therefore, the color variable, which contains the integers corresponding to the background colour, will be compared to the integer value of red by the expression `color == Color.RED`. If they are equal, this means that the background is currently red and will be changed to blue when the button is clicked. Else, the background is currently blue and will be changed to red when the user clicks the button.

Combining all these code lines, we reach the button listener method shown in Code 5.6.

```
public void myButtonListenerMethod() {
button = (Button) findViewById(R.id.button);
button.setOnClickListener(new
 View.OnClickListener() {
 @Override
  public void onClick(View v) {
   RelativeLayout bgElement = (RelativeLayout)
      findViewById(R.id.activity_main);
   int color = ((ColorDrawable)
   bgElement.getBackground()).getColor();
   if (color == Color.RED) {
     bgElement.setBackgroundColor(Color.BLUE);
           }
   else {
     bgElement.setBackgroundColor(Color.RED);
           }
         }
```

BEGINNER'S GUIDE TO ANDROID APP DEVELOPMENT

```
        });
}
```
Code 5.6 (cont'd from the previous page)

✓ Please note that we could use the if–else statement without curly
  brackets since there are only one line codes inside their blocks.
  However, I have written them with brackets for the sake of
  completeness.

We now have to call this button listener method when the activity is first
created. Therefore, we have to call it inside the onCreate() method as
follows:

```
protected void onCreate(Bundle savedInstanceState)
{
    super.onCreate(savedInstanceState);
    setContentView(R.layout.activity_main);
    myButtonListenerMethod();
}
```
Code 5.7

However, we are not done yet because the background is transparent by
default when an activity is first created. Therefore, we have to set it to
red or blue on creation. Let's set it as red by improving Code 5.7 as
follows:

```
protected void onCreate(Bundle savedInstanceState)
{
    super.onCreate(savedInstanceState);
    setContentView(R.layout.activity_main);
    RelativeLayout bgElement = (RelativeLayout)
      findViewById(R.id.activity_main);
    bgElement.setBackgroundColor(Color.RED);
    myButtonListenerMethod();
}
```
Code 5.8

In this code, the background is accessed and then set as red at the start of
the app. Please note that we need to define a separate bgElement object
inside the onCreate() method; we can't use the bgElement defined
inside the button listener method. This is because all variables and

objects declared in a method are valid only inside that method (also called as **scope of variables**).

Now, let's combine these code lines to form our complete MainActivity.java file as follows:

```
public class MainActivity extends
AppCompatActivity {

    Button button;
    @Override
    protected void onCreate(Bundle
        savedInstanceState) {
  super.onCreate(savedInstanceState);
  setContentView(R.layout.activity_main);
  RelativeLayout bgElement = (RelativeLayout)
        findViewById(R.id.activity_main);
  bgElement.setBackgroundColor(Color.WHITE);
  myButtonListenerMethod();
    }

public void myButtonListenerMethod() {
    button = (Button)findViewById(R.id.button);
    button.setOnClickListener(new
      View.OnClickListener() {
      @Override
  public void onClick(View v) {
    RelativeLayout bgElement =
  (RelativeLayout)findViewById(R.id.activity_main);
    int color = ((ColorDrawable)
    bgElement.getBackground()).getColor();
   if (color == Color.RED) {
    bgElement.setBackgroundColor(Color.BLUE);
    }
    else {
    bgElement.setBackgroundColor(Color.RED);
                }
            }
        });
    }
}
```
Code 5.9

5.4. Building and Running the App

We have completed both the layout and code development of our first Android app. Let's run it by clicking the **Run** button in Android Studio. I selected a Nexus 4 emulator for running our app on it. The emulator screen when the app is launched is shown in Figure 5.22.

Figure 5.22. The app when it is launched (colour and full resolution figure at the book's companion website: www.yamaclis.com/android)

As we click on the **Change!** Button, the background colour changes from red to blue and vice versa as shown in Figure 5.23. We can run this app on a real device as explained in Chapter 3 in detail. I tried this app on an Asus Zenfone 6 and it runs as expected on a real device too.

I hope you enjoyed developing our first programmatic Android app development. If there are question marks about the codes, don't worry, I'm sure you'll get used to Android coding in the upcoming chapters.

➢ **A simple exercise:** Could you modify the code to change the label of the button according to the background colour dynamically? If the background colour will be changed to blue, the button text will be **Convert to blue!** otherwise **Convert to red!**

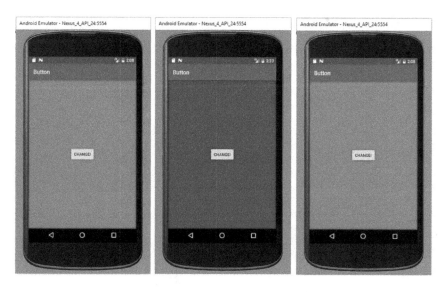

Figure 5.23. Our app's screen after subsequent button clicks (colour and full resolution figure at the book's companion website:
www.yamaclis.com/android)

ANDRIOD APP#2: BODY MASS INDEX (BMI) CALCULATOR

6.1. General Information

Body mass index (BMI) is a figure of merit that is used for assessing the thickness-thinness of a person. BMI is defined as the ratio of the mass and height-squared with the formula below:

$$BMI = \frac{mass\,(kg)}{(height\,(m))^2}$$

After the calculation of the BMI, the following table is the used for assessing the weight category:

Weight category	from BMI	to BMI
Very severely underweight	0	15
Severely underweight	15	16
Underweight	16	18.5
Normal (healthy weight)	18.5	25
Overweight	25	30
Obese Class I (Moderately obese)	30	35
Obese Class II (Severely obese)	35	40
Obese Class III (Very severely obese)	40	∞

Table 6.1. BMI categories
(source: https://en.wikipedia.org/wiki/Body_mass_index)

In this chapter, we'll develop a BMI calculator app and learn to read user inputs, make calculations inside our code and display results to the user.

6.2. Adding and Positioning TextViews

In order to calculate the BMI in our app, we obviously need the weight and height inputs. Our Java code will calculate the BMI using the given BMI formula and then it will decide the category according to Table 6.1. First of all, let's create the user interface of our app. In Android Studio, create a new project called "BMI Calculator" and save it anywhere you want on your computer (I'll not repeat myself about these things, we explained in detail in previous chapters). Please select the "Phone and Tablet" platforms with minimum SDK of API 15 as we did for the previous app. The default layout can be chosen as "Empty activity" with the main class being "MainActivity.java" and the layout file as "activity_main.xml". Please don't delete the default TextView of "Hello World" so that we can modify it to show our app title. Click on it and then it will be selected. Now, change its text as **BMI Calculator**, set its font size as 24sp and make the text bold as indicated by the numbers 1, 2 and 3 in Figure 6.1.

Let's position this title text so that it is positioned in the middle horizontally and has a distance of something like 50~60 dp from the top. (dp stands for Density Independent Pixel which is automatically adjusted when the display resolution is changed). For this, click on the **View all properties** as shown by 4 in Figure 6.1 and adjust the position of this TextView as shown in Figure 6.2. Please note that the horizontal middle guiding line is displayed automatically so that we can slide this widget on this line which will help us keep it in the middle horizontally. As you move the widget, observe the parameter named layout_marginT which indicates its distance from the top. I set it as 60 dp.

We'll take height and weight inputs from the user and show the BMI result as a number and its category. We'll need to place four TextViews which will show **Enter your weight (kg):** , **Enter your height (m):** , **Your BMI:** and **BMI category**. Please find the widget TextView from the Palette and drag and drop four TextViews as shown in Figure 6.3.

Figure 6.1. Setting the basic properties of the TextView (You can download full resolution colour images from the book's website)

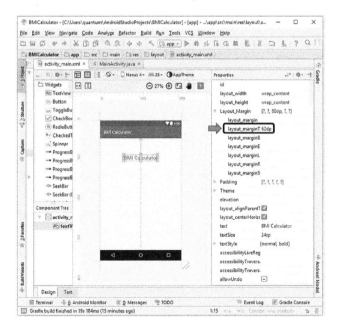

Figure 6.2. Positioning the title label

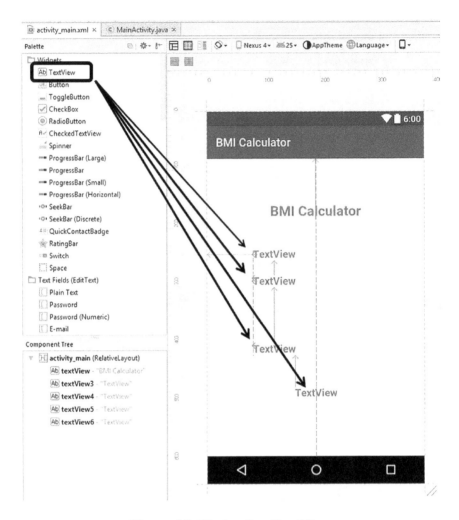

Figure 6.3. Placing four TextViews

Once the first TextView is placed, the next one is positioned relative to the previous one. For out BMI Calculator app, the exact positions are not strict and I am not giving the exact positions here in order to confuse you. You can download the project files from the book's companion website if you'd like to see which positions I exactly used but it is not mandatory of course. However, we need to leave a space between the second and the third TextViews for placing the button that will initiate the calculation.

I have changed the text font sizes to 18 sp and made the text type bold. The layout seems like in Figure 6.4 after changing the texts of these TextViews per our aim.

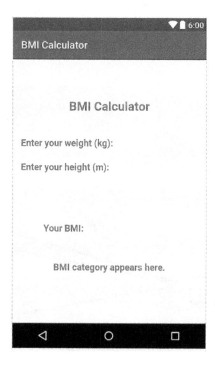

Figure 6.4. The app's GUI layout after setting up the TextViews

6.3. Adding the EditText Widgets

We now need to place two editable text boxes to let the user input his/her weight and height, another textbox to display the BMI as a number and a button to initiate the calculation of the BMI.

The positioning of the Text Fields (text boxes) are shown in Figure 6.5. I've placed Text Fields which can be used to input decimal numbers (numbers with fractional part) rather than general input types because the user is supposed to enter only numeric values in this app. It is worth noting that the calculation result will be displayed next to the **Your BMI:** label and a Text Field is placed there to display the BMI result. We could use a static text (TextView) for this aim however I wanted to show you how we can set the contents of the TextField programmatically.

Figure 6.5. Placing the TextFields

Please note that Text Fields do not have borders by default therefore after they are placed, we can only see them by selecting them.

Let's set their IDs so that we can access them programmatically and also set their default texts. For this, select the respective TextField and then set the ID and text properties as shown in Figure 6.6 for the weight input

Text Field. I also positioned its default text in the middle as we did before.

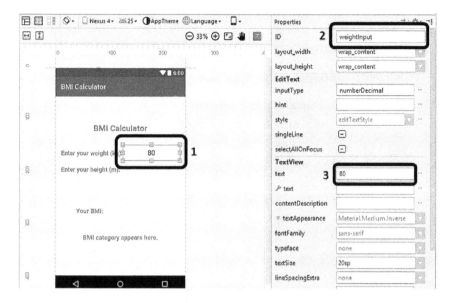

Figure 6.6. Settings of the weight input TextField

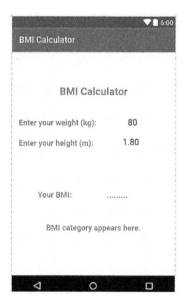

Figure 6.7. The GUI of the app after setting up all TextFields

Please set the IDs and default texts of the height input and BMI result Text Fields as **heightInput** and 1.80; **BMIResult** and ...., respectively. Bu setting the default text of the BMI result Text Field as ...., we make the user to see .... in that box before calculating his/her BMI. After these settings, the GUI seems as in Figure 6.7.

6.4. Adding and Positioning the Button

There are two steps remaining to complete our GUI design. The first one is the button that will initiate the calculation. Please drag and drop a button widget from the Palette between the height input TextView and the YourBMI TextView and then position it horizontally in the middle as shown below:

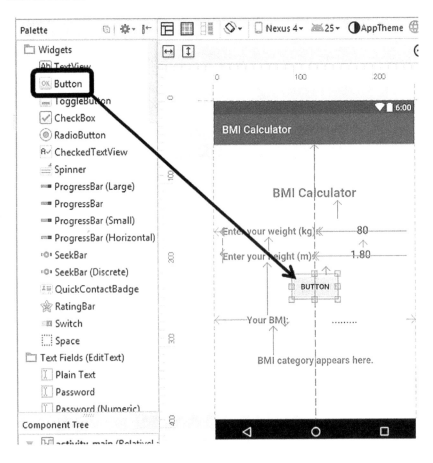

Figure 6.8. Placing the button on the screen

Now, please set the text of the button as **Calculate my BMI!** Note that the default ID of the button is **button** which is OK.

Our GUI is almost complete however there's one step remaining. The ID of the BMI category TextView (the one with the text **Your BMI category appears here.**). Please set its ID as **BMICategory** and then we are finished. After these steps, the GUI of our app is ready as shown below:

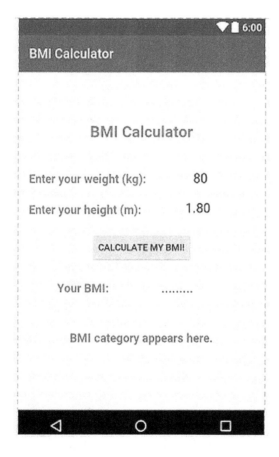

Figure 6.9. The GUI of our BMI Calculator app

6.5. Developing the Main Code of the App

We are now ready to continue with programming. We will implement the following steps in MainActivity.java for the BMI calculation:

➢ Firstly, the values entered in the weight input and height input text fields will be taken. These will be String type variables.
➢ Convert these Strings to double type variables so that the BMI calculation can be performed using the BMI equation given at the beginning of the chapter.
➢ Perform the body mass index calculation.
➢ Display the BMI value in the text field next to the "**Your BMI:**" label after converting to String type.
➢ Use if–else statements to determine the BMI category from the BMI value using Table 6.1.
➢ Display the BMI category in the text view which shows "**BMI category appears here.**" by default.

Please open the MainActivity.java file from the file explorer of Android Studio. The default contents of this file are as follows:

```
package com.helloworld.quantum.bmicalculator;

import android.support.v7.app.AppCompatActivity;
import android.os.Bundle;

public class MainActivity extends AppCompatActivity
{

    @Override
    protected void onCreate(Bundle savedInstanceState) {
        super.onCreate(savedInstanceState);
        setContentView(R.layout.activity_main);
    }
}
```
Code 6.1

The calculation will be done when the user taps the button therefore we need to write a listener method for the button and then call this method inside the `onCreate()` function (as we explained in the previous chapter). Code 6.2 shows the general template of the button listener method.

```
public void myButtonListenerMethod()  {

  Button button = (Button) findViewById(R.id.button);

  button.setOnClickListener(new View.OnClickListener() {
        @Override
        public void onClick(View v) {
// code those will be run when the button's clicked
        }
    });
}
```
Code 6.2

We have analysed the structure of this listener method in Chapter 5. In short, the button is accessed by the `button` object created in the second line and all the operations those will be done when the button is clicked will go inside the method `onClick(View v)`.

First of all we need to take the height and weight inputs from their respective EditTexts (TextFields). This is simply done with the following code snippet:

```
final EditText heightText = (EditText)
              findViewById(R.id.heightInput);

String  heightStr = heightText.getText().toString();
double height = Double.parseDouble(heightStr);
```
Code 6.3

The explanation of this code is as follows:

➢ In the first line, we access the height input textbox using its ID (`R.id.heightInput`) and then create an EditText object called `heightText`.

➢ In the second line, the string inside this EditText is extracted and assigned to a new String object called `heightStr`.

➢ And in the last line, the String value of the height is converted to double type and assigned to a newly created variable `height`.

➢ In the end, we have the height value stored in the `height` variable which is of double type.

We need to implement these steps because there's no other way to directly take the EditText value as a `String` or `double`.

The following code does a similar job and in the end the weight value is stored in the `weight` variable.

```
final EditText weightText = (EditText)
                findViewById(R.id.weightInput);

String  weightStr = weightText.getText().toString();
double weight = Double.parseDouble(heightStr);
```
Code 6.4

We now have weight and height data in double type variables so we can do the BMI calculation using the equation given in the beginning of the chapter as follows:

```
double BMI = (weight)/(height*height);
```
Code 6.5

In this code, the `*` operator does the multiplication while the `/` operator divides the weight to the height squared.

We will display this BMI value in the EditText box next to the **You BMI** label in the GUI. We did set its ID as **BMIResult** when we laid out the user interface before. Therefore, the following code does this job:

```
final EditText BMIResult = (EditText)
                findViewById(R.id.BMIResult);

BMIResult.setText(Double.toString(BMI));
```
Code 6.6

In this code, the widget with the ID **BMIResult** is found in the first line and then the double type BMI variable is converted to String by the code `Double.toString(BMI)` for displaying inside the EditText. Note that the texts written inside the EditText widgets can only be read and written as Strings.

We now have the BMI stored as a double type variable. We now have to use if–else statements to check this numeric value according to Table 6.1

and determine the BMI category. For this, let's define a String that will hold the BMI category:

```
String BMI_Cat;
```
Code 6.7

We'll set this String according to the BMI value using if–else statements as follows:

```
if (BMI < 15)
    BMI_Cat = "Very severely underweight";
else if (BMI < 16)
    BMI_Cat = "Severely underweight";
else if (BMI < 18.5)
    BMI_Cat = "Underweight";
else if (BMI < 25)
    BMI_Cat = "Normal";
else if (BMI < 30)
    BMI_Cat = "Overweight";
else if (BMI < 35)
    BMI_Cat = "Obese Class 1 - Moderately Obese";
else if (BMI < 40)
    BMI_Cat = "Obese Class 2 - Severely Obese";
else
    BMI_Cat = "Obese Class 3 - Very Severely Obese";
```
Code 6.8

The only thing remaining is setting the TextView to the BMI_Cat String so that the BMI category is displayed in the user interface:

```
final TextView BMICategory = (TextView)
                findViewById(R.id.BMICategory);
BMICategory.setText(BMI_Cat);
```
Code 6.9

Sticking all these code lines together, we reach the complete MainActivity.java given in Code 6.10. (**You can download these codes from the book's website:** www.yamaclis.com/android)

Please note that the library import directives at the beginning of this file are automatically placed by Android Studio according to the methods and classes we used in our code.

```
package com.helloworld.quantum.bmicalculator;

import android.graphics.Color;
import android.graphics.drawable.ColorDrawable;
import android.support.v7.app.AppCompatActivity;
import android.os.Bundle;
import android.view.View;
import android.widget.Button;
import android.widget.EditText;
import android.widget.RelativeLayout;
import android.widget.TextView;

public class MainActivity extends AppCompatActivity
{

    @Override
 protected void onCreate(Bundle savedInstanceState)
{
        super.onCreate(savedInstanceState);
        setContentView(R.layout.activity_main);
        myButtonListenerMethod();
    }

public void myButtonListenerMethod() {
  Button button = (Button)findViewById(R.id.button);
  button.setOnClickListener(new
       View.OnClickListener() {
  @Override
  public void onClick(View v) {
    final EditText heightText = (EditText)
    findViewById(R.id.heightInput);
String  heightStr = heightText.getText().toString();
double height = Double.parseDouble(heightStr);
final EditText weightText = (EditText)
    findViewById(R.id.weightInput);
String weightStr = weightText.getText().toString();
double weight = Double.parseDouble(weightStr);
double BMI = (weight)/(height*height);
final EditText BMIResult = (EditText)
    findViewById(R.id.BMIResult);
BMIResult.setText(Double.toString(BMI));
String BMI_Cat;
    if (BMI < 15)
        BMI_Cat = "Very severely underweight";
    else if (BMI < 16)
        BMI_Cat = "Severely underweight";
    else if (BMI < 18.5)
```

```
      BMI_Cat = "Underweight";
  else if (BMI < 25)
    BMI_Cat = "Normal";
  else if (BMI < 30)
    BMI_Cat = "Overweight";
  else if (BMI < 35)
    BMI_Cat = "Obese Class 1 - Moderately Obese";
  else if (BMI < 40)
    BMI_Cat = "Obese Class 2 - Severely Obese";
  else
   BMI_Cat = "Obese Class 3 - Very Severely Obese";

  final TextView BMICategory = (TextView)
          findViewById(R.id.BMICategory);
  BMICategory.setText(BMI_Cat);
         }
     });
  }
}
```

Code 6.10 (cont'd from the previous page)

6.6. Building and Running the App

Let's now try our app in the Nexus 4 emulator. Just press the "Run" button in Android Studio and select the Nexus 4 emulator. You should see the app screen shown in Figure 6.10.

Enter weight and height values (in kg and metres) and then tap the **CALCULATE MY BMI!** button. If you followed all steps correctly, you should see the BMI value and the BMI category on your app screen as in Figure 6.11.

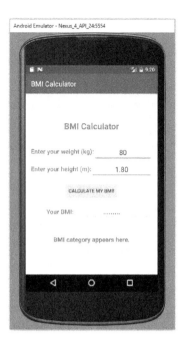

Figure 6.10. The app screen

Figure 6.11. A sample BMI calculation

6.7. Final Notes

As you can see from Figure 6.11, the BMI value is displayed with a lot of unnecessary floating point digits. Probably only a single decimal digit is enough. We can use the following code to trim the decimal digits of the BMI variable and assign the trimmed value to a new double type variable BMI_trimmed:

```
DecimalFormat df = new DecimalFormat("#.#");
double BMI_trimmed =
            Double.parseDouble(df.format(BMI));
```
Code 6.11

The DecimalFormat class is used for these types of operations. Android Studio automatically adds the required library by the code line:

```
import android.icu.text.DecimalFormat;
```
Code 6.12

The modified complete MainActivity.java is also given as follows:

```
package com.helloworld.quantum.bmicalculator;

import android.graphics.Color;
import android.graphics.drawable.ColorDrawable;
import android.support.v7.app.AppCompatActivity;
import android.os.Bundle;
import android.view.View;
import android.widget.Button;
import android.widget.EditText;
import android.widget.RelativeLayout;
import android.widget.TextView;

public class MainActivity extends AppCompatActivity
{

    @Override
protected void onCreate(Bundle savedInstanceState) {
    super.onCreate(savedInstanceState);
    setContentView(R.layout.activity_main);
    myButtonListenerMethod();
      }

public void myButtonListenerMethod() {
Button button = (Button)findViewById(R.id.button);
```

```
button.setOnClickListener(new
   View.OnClickListener() {
   @Override
public void onClick(View v) {

    final EditText heightText = (EditText)
         findViewById(R.id.heightInput);
    String  heightStr =
         heightText.getText().toString();
    double height = Double.parseDouble(heightStr);

    final EditText weightText = (EditText)
         findViewById(R.id.weightInput);
    String weightStr =
         weightText.getText().toString();
    double weight = Double.parseDouble(weightStr);

    double BMI = (weight)/(height*height);
    DecimalFormat df = new DecimalFormat("#.#");
    double BMI_trimmed =
    Double.parseDouble(df.format(BMI));
    final EditText BMIResult = (EditText)
    findViewById(R.id.BMIResult);
    BMIResult.setText(Double.toString(BMI_trimmed));

    String BMI_Cat;

    if (BMI < 15)
         BMI_Cat = "Very severely underweight";
    else if (BMI < 16)
         BMI_Cat = "Severely underweight";
    else if (BMI < 18.5)
         BMI_Cat = "Underweight";
    else if (BMI < 25)
         BMI_Cat = "Normal";
    else if (BMI < 30)
         BMI_Cat = "Overweight";
    else if (BMI < 35)
         BMI_Cat = "Obese Class 1 - Moderately
                    Obese";
     else if (BMI < 40)
         BMI_Cat = "Obese Class 2 - Severely Obese";
     else
         BMI_Cat = "Obese Class 3 - Very Severely
                    Obese";
 final TextView BMICategory = (TextView)
                 findViewById(R.id.BMICategory);
```

```
    BMICategory.setText(BMI_Cat);
            }
        });
    }
}
```

Code 6.13 (cont'd from the previous page)

When the modified code is used, the calculation result is displayed in the emulator as follows:

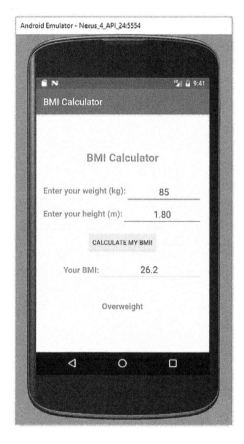

Figure 6.12. The sample BMI calculation with trimmed BMI digits

Note 2. I have verified that our BMI Calculator app works as expected on a real device (Asus Zenfone 6).

Note 3. Don't worry if the app categorizes you obese, it does me too (the values shown in Figure 6.12 are not mine☺). Please consult your doctor and dietician for the ways of decreasing your BMI like regularly exercising and eating less processed food.

We'll develop a dice rolling app in the next chapter where you will learn adding dynamic images to your app and utilizing randomness functions in Android. See you after a strong coffee!

ANDRIOD APP #3: SIMPLE DICE ROLLER

7.1. Creating the Project and Adding an Imageview Widget

We'll develop a simple dice rolling app in this chapter. We'll learn how to use images in the GUI and also code for basic random number generation in Java for rolling a virtual dice. When we hit a **Roll** button, the app will choose a number between 1 and 6 randomly, show the result as a number in a TextView and also display a dice image that shows the outcome.

Please create a new project and save it on your computer. Select an empty activity as usual. I named my project as **Dice Roller** but you can of course give any name you'd like.

First of all, let's design the user interface. While the activity_main.xml file is opened in Android Studio, please change the default Textview's text from **Hello World** to **Dice Roller** and position it on the top of the GUI aligned horizontally in the middle as shown in Figure 7.1.

We now need to place an ImageView component which will be used to display the dice face images. However, we first need to import the image files to the project. When the app first starts, it is good to show a generic dice image and then change the image to the respective dice face image when the user rolls the dice. For this, we need to insert a general dice image and 6 dice face images to Android Studio. These images are shown in Figure 7.2 which can be downloaded from the book's companion website www.yamaclis.com/android.

Figure 7.1. TextView showing the title of the app

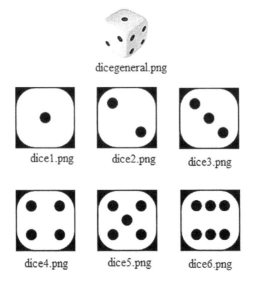

Figure 7.2. Dice face images and their filenames used in the app

Please select and right-click → copy all of these images in the file explorer of your computer (just as you do when you select files for copy-paste) and then right-click → paste in the **drawable** folder in Android Studio as shown below:

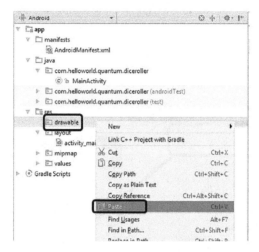

Figure 7.3. Adding image files to the Android Studio project

When we click the arrow symbol just at the left of **drawable** folder, we can see the newly added image files as in Figure 7.4.

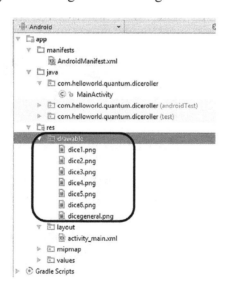

Figure 7.4. The image files imported in the project

Let's place the ImageView object to the GUI now. Please find the ImageView object in the Palette and drag and drop to the app's layout as follows:

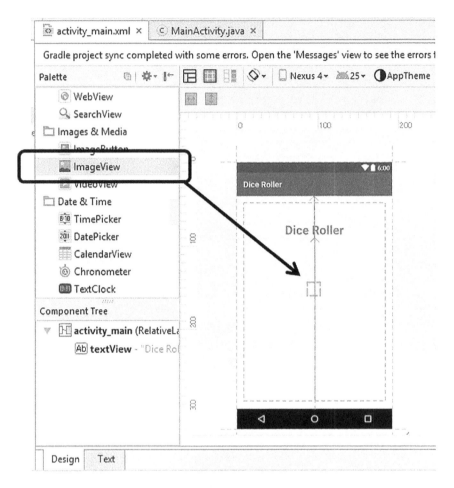

Figure 7.5. Adding an ImageView object

When we drop the ImageView on the GUI, Android Studio wants us to set its image as in Figure 7.6. The selected image will be the image shown inside the ImageView when the app first starts (i.e. default image). Therefore, please select the dicegeneral.png as in Figure 7.6.

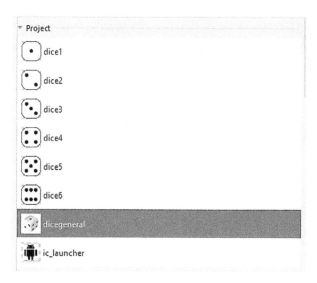

Figure 7.6. Selecting the default image for the ImageView

After this selection, press OK and then the layout of our app will be shown as follows:

Figure 7.7. The layout after placing the ImageView

7.2. Adding the Other Widgets and Setting up the IDs

Please place a TextView and a Button just below the ImageView object which will display the result of the rolling and initiate the rolling, respectively. I have set the TextView to show **Please tap the button...**. Similarly, the button's text is changed to **ROLL!** as shown below:

Figure 7.8. The GUI after placing all of the required objects

We'll need the IDs of the dice image, the result TextView and the button because we'll access them in the code. I've assigned their IDs as **diceImage**, **rollResult** and **rollButton**, respectively.

7.3. Developing the Main Code of the App

Let's start coding a button listener method which will be called when the user taps the **Roll!** button. The template of the button listener is as shown in Code 7.1 (as we developed in previous chapters). In this method, a Button object called **button** is declared and the button on the GUI is accessed via this object. Then, the clicks on this button is listened by the `setOnClickListener()` method. The procedures those will be run when the button's clicked will go inside the `onClick()` method as usual.

```
public void myButtonListenerMethod() {
Button button = (Button) findViewById(R.id.rollButton);
    button.setOnClickListener(new
                        View.OnClickListener() {
        @Override
        public void onClick(View v) {
    });
}
```
Code 7.1

We need to utilize a method to generate random numbers between 1 and 6. There are various randomness methods in Java. The following Random object does the job for our simple dice roller:

```
Random rand = new Random();
int rollResult = rand.nextInt(6) + 1;
```
Code 7.2

In this code, a **Random** object called `rand` is created in the first line. In the second line, the method `nextInt()` is applied on this object by `rand.nextInt(6)`. The `nextInt(int n)` method generates random numbers between 0 and n–1 therefore `rand.nextInt(6)` generates random numbers between 0 and 5. Therefore the expression `rand.nextInt(6) + 1` gives random numbers between 1 and 6 for simulating a dice. This random number is assigned to the integer variable `rollResult`.

We'll display the `rollResult` integer in the `diceResult` TextView on the user interface. In the following code, a TextView object is created to access the `diceResult` TextView and then its text is set as `Integer.toString(rollResult)` which is the String expression of `rollResult`:

```
TextView diceResult = (TextView)
        findViewById(R.id.diceResult);
diceResult.setText(Integer.toString(rollResult));
```
Code 7.3

The last thing we need to add is the code to change the ImageView's image according to the rolling result. Firstly, we will access the ImageView object using the following code line:

```
ImageView img = (ImageView)
                findViewById(R.id.diceImage);
```
Code 7.4

Since the rolling result is an integer number, we can easily utilize the switch–case statements to change the image as follows:

```
switch (rollResult) {
    case 1:
        img.setImageResource(R.drawable.dice1);
        break;
    case 2:
        img.setImageResource(R.drawable.dice2);
        break;
    case 3:
        img.setImageResource(R.drawable.dice3);
        break;
    case 4:
        img.setImageResource(R.drawable.dice4);
        break;
    case 5:
        img.setImageResource(R.drawable.dice5);
        break;
    case 6:
        img.setImageResource(R.drawable.dice6);
        break;
}
```
Code 7.5

Please note that we change the image of the `ImageView` object `img` with the method `setImageResource()` which takes the image resource with the template `R.drawable."imagename"`.

Combining all these code lines and calling the button listener method inside the `onCreate()` method of the activity, we reach the complete MainActivity.java given below:

```
package com.helloworld.quantum.myapplication;
import android.support.v7.app.AppCompatActivity;
import android.os.Bundle;
```

```java
import android.view.View;
import android.widget.Button;
import android.widget.EditText;
import android.widget.ImageView;
import android.widget.TextView;
import java.util.Random;

public class MainActivity extends AppCompatActivity
{

    @Override
    protected void onCreate(Bundle savedInstanceState) {

        super.onCreate(savedInstanceState);
        setContentView(R.layout.activity_main);
        myButtonListenerMethod();
    }

public void myButtonListenerMethod() {
        Button button = (Button)
            findViewById(R.id.rollButton);

button.setOnClickListener(new View.OnClickListener()
{
            @Override
        public void onClick(View v) {
        Random rand = new Random();
        int rollResult = rand.nextInt(6) + 1;

        TextView diceResult = (TextView)
            findViewById(R.id.diceResult);

diceResult.setText(Integer.toString(rollResult));

        ImageView img = (ImageView)
            findViewById(R.id.diceImage);

  switch (rollResult) {
    case 1:
        img.setImageResource(R.drawable.dice1);
        break;
    case 2:
        img.setImageResource(R.drawable.dice2);
        break;
    case 3:
        img.setImageResource(R.drawable.dice3);
        break;
```

```
    case 4:
       img.setImageResource(R.drawable.dice4);
       break;
    case 5:
       img.setImageResource(R.drawable.dice5);
       break;
    case 6:
       img.setImageResource(R.drawable.dice6);
       break;
                      }
                 }
           });
       }
}
```

Code 7.6 (cont'd from the previous page)

7.4. Building and Running the App

Let's run our dice roller app by hitting the "Run" button in Android Studio and selecting an emulator such as Nexus 4 as we did before. The app shown in Figure 7.9 appears. Each time you click the ROLL! button, the app should show a different number with the corresponding die face image as in Figure 7.10. The app also works properly on a real device as it should.

It is worth noting that random numbers are not only used for fun apps but also in everyday cryptographic processes like online credit card transactions, etc. Hence there are much more sophisticated random number generation functions in Java and Android, also with the aid of external libraries. However for simple randomness like in our die rolling game, the Random class seems adequate. You can check its randomness by consecutively clicking on the **Roll!** button and observing if you obtain the same number a lot or if the numbers show a pattern that you can guess the next number. However please keep in mind that accurate testing of randomness requires complex tools.

Let's take a short break before continuing to the next chapter where we'll develop a compass app which will utilize the internal accelerometer and magnetometer sensor of the device.

Figure 7.9. The app when it is first run

Figure 7.10. The app showing 6 after one of its rolling

Chapter 8

ANDROID APP #4: THE COMPASS

We'll develop a simple compass app that will utilize the internal accelerometer and magnetometer sensors of the Android device. Accelerometer is a sensor which converts the mechanical acceleration information to electrical signals and similarly a magnetometer is used to translate the magnetic field intensity to electronic signals.

Most Android devices have an accelerometer and a magnetometer sensor inside therefore using a compass app only requires software rather than additional hardware.

As we develop our compass app, we'll learn setting permissions to use sensors, reading acceleration and magnetic field data in Java code, extracting the orientation data from the sensor data and animating images. In the end, we'll have a complete compass app that we can use in daily life.

8.1. Setting up the Required Permissions

Let's start by creating an Android project first. I named the project as **Compass App** and selected **Empty Activity** as the default activity type. The minimum API is also set to 15.

We'll need a compass image whose needle shows the absolute north. I found the royalty free image shown in Figure 8.1 for this aim (I chose this one because it looks sort of ancient like an ancient compass ☺). You can download this image from the book's companion website as usual. You can of course use any other image you like in your project. Please copy and paste this image to your drawable folder as we did before. The name of the image is compass.png, we'll use its name to access it in our code.

Figure 8.1. The compass image

If we use sensors in an Android project, we have to get the required permissions to use these sensors in the AndroidManifest.xml file which is located in the **manifests** folder as shown below:

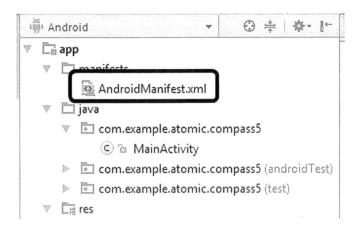

Figure 8.2. The AndroidManifest file in the project explorer

Open this file by double clicking on it in Android Studio and you'll see its default contents as shown in Figure 8.3. Please add the lines shown in Code 8.1 to this file before the `<application>` tag and you'll obtain the finalized contents as shown in Code 8.2. These lines make the accelerometer and magnetometer outputs available to be used in our app.

```
activity_main.xml ×    © MainActivity.java ×    AndroidManifest.xml ×

  manifest   application   activity   intent-filter   category

  <?xml version="1.0" encoding="utf-8"?>
  <manifest xmlns:android="http://schemas.android.com/apk/res/android"
      package="com.example.atomic.compassapp">

      <application
          android:allowBackup="true"
          android:icon="@mipmap/ic_launcher"
          android:label="Compass App"
          android:supportsRtl="true"
          android:theme="@style/AppTheme">
          <activity android:name=".MainActivity">
              <intent-filter>
                  <action android:name="android.intent.action.MAIN" />

                  <category android:name="android.intent.category.LAUNCHER" />
              </intent-filter>
          </activity>
      </application>

  </manifest>
```

Figure 8.3. Default contents of the AndroidManifest.xml file

```
<uses-feature
android:name="android.hardware.sensor.accelerometer"
android:required="true" />

<uses-feature
android:name="android.hardware.sensor.magnetometer"
android:required="true" />
```
Code 8.1

```
<?xml version="1.0" encoding="utf-8"?>
<manifest
xmlns:android="http://schemas.android.com/apk/res/and
roid"
    package="com.example.atomic.compassapp">
<uses-feature
android:name="android.hardware.sensor.accelerometer"
android:required="true" />
<uses-feature
android:name="android.hardware.sensor.magnetometer"
android:required="true" />
    <application
        android:allowBackup="true"
        android:icon="@mipmap/ic_launcher"
        android:label="@string/app_name"
```

```
            android:supportsRtl="true"
            android:theme="@style/AppTheme">
            <activity android:name=".MainActivity">
                <intent-filter>
                    <action
android:name="android.intent.action.MAIN" />

                    <category
android:name="android.intent.category.LAUNCHER" />
                </intent-filter>
            </activity>
        </application>

</manifest>
```
Code 8.2 (cont'd from the pervious page)

8.2. Designing the GUI of the App

Now, let's design the layout of the app. Please open the layout_main.xml file for this and change the text of the default **Hello World** TextView to **Compass App** which will serve as the app title. Please set its font size as 30sp and bold style. Then, please position it as follows:

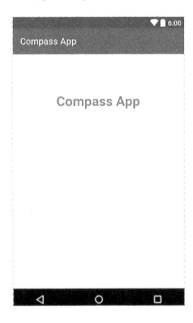

Figure 8.4. The TextView used to display the title of the app

Let's now place an ImageView in the middle of the GUI and select the compass image that we pasted to the drawable folder:

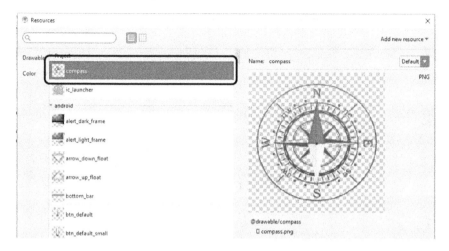

Figure 8.5. Selecting the compass image for the ImageView component

After we place the ImageView, it'll be selected. Then, please set up its ID as **iv_compass** (short for ImageView_compass) from the right pane of Android Studio as follows:

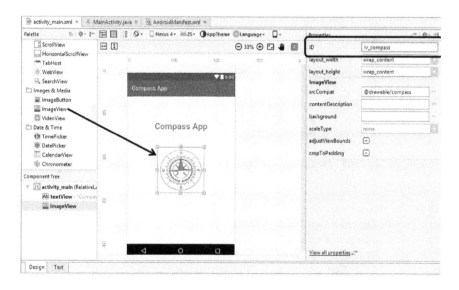

Figure 8.6. Setting the ID of the compass ImageView

Finally, let's place a TextView below the ImageView in which we'll display the orientation angle in real time. I set its ID as **tv_degrees** (short for TextView_degrees), and made it 24sp with a bold text as shown below:

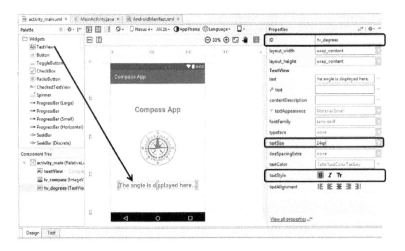

Figure 8.7. Adding the TextView to display the orientation angle

8.3. Writing the Main Code of the App

We completed the design of the user interface and now ready to continue with the coding. Please open the MainActivity.java file in Android Studio. This file will have the default contents as follows:

```java
package com.example.atomic.compassapp;

import android.support.v7.app.AppCompatActivity;
import android.os.Bundle;

public class MainActivity extends AppCompatActivity
{

    @Override
    protected void onCreate(Bundle
savedInstanceState) {
        super.onCreate(savedInstanceState);
        setContentView(R.layout.activity_main);
    }
}
```
Code 8.3

The horizontal direction of a compass bearing is called as azimuth. We'll calculate this angle from the magnetometer and accelerometer outputs. Let's define a **float** type variable to hold this data:

```
Float azimuth_angle;
```
Code 8.4

We also need to define objects related to the sensors as follows:

```
private SensorManager compassSensorManager;
Sensor accelerometer;
Sensor magnetometer;
```
Code 8.5

In this code, the first object is a **SensorManager** object that is used to access the sensors. The other two declarations define **Sensor** objects for reading the outputs of the accelerometer and the magnetometer.

Finally, let's declare ImageView and TextView objects which will be used to access the corresponding components in the GUI:

```
TextView tv_degrees;
ImageView iv_compass;
```
Code 8.6

We can place these declarations inside the **MainActivity** class just before the **onCreate()** method. Then, we can assign the default accelerometer and magnetometer sensors to their objects inside the **onCreate()** method as follows:

```
compassSensorManager =
(SensorManager)getSystemService(SENSOR_SERVICE);

accelerometer =
compassSensorManager.getDefaultSensor(Sensor.TYPE_ACC
ELEROMETER);

magnetometer =
compassSensorManager.getDefaultSensor(Sensor.TYPE_MAG
NETIC_FIELD);
```
Code 8.7

After these declarations and assignments, the MainActivity.java file currently looks like Code 8.8.

```
package com.example.atomic.compassapp;

import android.hardware.Sensor;
import android.hardware.SensorManager;
import android.support.v7.app.AppCompatActivity;
import android.os.Bundle;
import android.widget.ImageView;
import android.widget.TextView;

public class MainActivity extends AppCompatActivity {

    Float azimuth_angle;
    private SensorManager compassSensorManager;
    Sensor accelerometer;
    Sensor magnetometer;
    TextView tv_degrees;
    ImageView iv_compass;

    @Override
    protected void onCreate(Bundle
      savedInstanceState) {
        super.onCreate(savedInstanceState);
        setContentView(R.layout.activity_main);
        compassSensorManager =
    (SensorManager)getSystemService(SENSOR_SERVICE);
    accelerometer = compassSensorManager
      .getDefaultSensor(Sensor.TYPE_ACCELEROMETER);
    magnetometer = compassSensorManager
      .getDefaultSensor(Sensor.TYPE_MAGNETIC_FIELD);
    }
}
```
Code 8.8

In order to continue with reading sensors, we have to implement
SensorEventListener class. We do this by using the **implements**
keyword in the main class definition as follows:

```
public class MainActivity extends AppCompatActivity
    implements SensorEventListener
```
Code 8.9

Note that this is a single line code.

When we implement **SensorEventListener** class, Android Studio warns
us by a red bulb saying that we need to implement the required methods in our
code:

Figure 8.8. Warning for implementing the required methods

Please click the **Implement methods** and then Android Studio will automatically place the **onSensorChanged()** and **onSensorActivityChanged()** methods when we click the **OK** button in the dialog box:

Figure 8.9. Dialog showing the methods which will be implemented

Android Studio automatically places the following code to MainActivity.java:

```
@Override
public void onSensorChanged(SensorEvent event) {

}

@Override
public void onAccuracyChanged(Sensor sensor, int
accuracy) {

}
```
Code 8.10

We'll write our main code inside the `onSensorChanged()` method. However, before moving on to the main code, let's write the `onResume()` and `onPause()` methods for the main activity because sensors are power hungry components therefore it is important to pause and resume the sensor listeners when the activity pauses and resumes. For this, we simply add the following code just below the end of the `onCreate()` method:

```
protected void onResume() {
    super.onResume();
    mSensorManager.registerListener(this,
accelerometer, SensorManager.SENSOR_DELAY_UI);
    mSensorManager.registerListener(this,
magnetometer, SensorManager.SENSOR_DELAY_UI);
}

protected void onPause() {
    super.onPause();
    mSensorManager.unregisterListener(this);
}
```
Code 8.11

In the `onResume()` method, the sensor listeners are registered meaning that the sensors are powered on again when the activity resumes. Similarly, the sensors are unregistered (disconnected) in the `onPause()` method when the activity pauses.

We're now ready to write the main code. Firstly, let's define two `float` type arrays to hold the accelerometer and magnetometer output data. These will be array variables because the outputs of these sensors are vectoral quantities i.e. they have different values for different directions.

We can define the arrays named `accel_read` and `magnetic_read` for these sensors as follows:

```
float[] accel_read;
float[] magnetic_read;
```
Code 8.12

Please write these declarations just before the `onSensorChanged()` method so that we can access these variables from anywhere in the `onSensorChanged()` method.

Inside the `onSensorChanged()` method: This method is called automatically when there's a new sensor event therefore we'll write our main code inside this method. The following code creates objects to access the ImageView and TextView of the GUI which will be updated when a sensor event happens:

```
tv_degrees =(TextView) findViewById(R.id.tv_degrees);
iv_compass = (ImageView) findViewById(R.id.iv_compass);
```
Code 8.13

Then, the following code reads accelerometer and magnetometer sensors and stores the output data to `accel_read` and `magnetic_read` arrays:

```
if (event.sensor.getType() == Sensor.TYPE_ACCELEROMETER)
    accel_read = event.values;
if (event.sensor.getType() == Sensor.TYPE_MAGNETIC_FIELD)
    magnetic_read = event.values;
```
Code 8.14

If the sensor outputs are available (i.e. they are not null), we'll use the `accel_read` and `magnetic_read` variables in the method called `getRotationMatrix()` to get the rotation matrix `R` of the device as follows:

```
if (accel_read != null && magnetic_read != null) {
    float R[] = new float[9];
    float I[] = new float[9];
    boolean successful_read = SensorManager
     .getRotationMatrix(R, I, accel_read,
      magnetic_read);
```
Code 8.15

If this operation is successful, the `successful_read` variable will be `true` and the rotation matrix will be stored in the variable R. In this case, we're ready to get the azimuth angle (the angle between the device direction and the absolute north) as follows:

```
if (successsful_read) {
    float orientation[] = new float[3];
    SensorManager.getOrientation(R, orientation);
    azimuth_angle = orientation[0];
    float degrees = ((azimuth_angle * 180f) / 3.14f);
    int degreesInt = Math.round(degrees);
    tv_degrees.setText(Integer.toString(degreesInt) +
      (char) 0x00B0 + " to absolute north.");
}
```
Code 8.16

In this code:

➢ A new array called `orientation` is declared.
➢ The orientation of the device is extracted using the `getOrientation()` method and 3-dimensional orientation data is stored in the `orientation` array.
➢ The first component of this array is the azimuth angle in radians, which is assigned to the `azimuth_angle` variable in the fourth line.
➢ In the fifth line, the azimuth angle in radians is converted to degrees and assigned to the newly created variable `degrees`.
➢ The degrees variable is of `float` type therefore it is better to round it to an `integer`. The sixth code line does this job using the method `Math.round()`.
➢ Finally, the azimuth angle in integer degrees is shown in the TextView in the user interface. The char 0x00B0 is used to display the degree symbol (°).

It is also good to rotate the compass image according to the azimuth angle. For this animation, we need to declare a `float` type variable which will hold the current value of the ImageView's rotation degree:

```
private float current_degree = 0f;
```
Code 8.17

Then, we can use the following animation code which will rotate the ImageView according to the azimuth angle:

```
RotateAnimation rotate = new
RotateAnimation(current_degree, -degreesInt,
Animation.RELATIVE_TO_SELF, 0.5f,
Animation.RELATIVE_TO_SELF, 0.5f);
rotate.setDuration(100);
rotate.setFillAfter(true);

iv_compass.startAnimation(rotate);
current_degree = -degreesInt;
```
Code 8.18

In this code, we declared a `RotateAnimate` object and then set the animation duration. The `startAnimation` starts the rotation of the ImageView. This code rotates the compass image in real time according to the `degreesInt` variable which holds the azimuth angle data.

Combining all these code lines, we reach the following MainActivity.java shown below:

```
package com.example.atomic.compassapp;
import android.hardware.Sensor;
import android.hardware.SensorEvent;
import android.hardware.SensorEventListener;
import android.hardware.SensorManager;
import android.support.v7.app.AppCompatActivity;
import android.os.Bundle;
import android.view.animation.Animation;
import android.view.animation.RotateAnimation;
import android.widget.ImageView;
import android.widget.TextView;

public class MainActivity extends AppCompatActivity
implements SensorEventListener {
    Float azimuth_angle;
    private SensorManager compassSensorManager;
    Sensor accelerometer;
    Sensor magnetometer;
    TextView tv_degrees;
    ImageView iv_compass;
    private float current_degree = 0f;
```

```java
@Override
protected void onCreate(Bundle savedInstanceState) {
    super.onCreate(savedInstanceState);
    setContentView(R.layout.activity_main);

    compassSensorManager = (SensorManager)
        .getSystemService(SENSOR_SERVICE);

    accelerometer = compassSensorManager
        .getDefaultSensor(Sensor.TYPE_ACCELEROMETER);

    magnetometer = compassSensorManager
        .getDefaultSensor(Sensor.TYPE_MAGNETIC_FIELD);
}

protected void onResume() {
    super.onResume();
    compassSensorManager.registerListener(this,
        accelerometer, SensorManager.SENSOR_DELAY_UI);

    compassSensorManager.registerListener(this,
        magnetometer, SensorManager.SENSOR_DELAY_UI);
}

protected void onPause() {
    super.onPause();

compassSensorManager.unregisterListener(this);
}

float[] accel_read;
float[] magnetic_read;
@Override
public void onSensorChanged(SensorEvent event) {
    tv_degrees =(TextView)
        findViewById(R.id.tv_degrees);
    iv_compass = (ImageView)
        findViewById(R.id.iv_compass);

    if (event.sensor.getType() == Sensor.TYPE_ACCELEROMETER)
        accel_read = event.values;
    if (event.sensor.getType() == Sensor.TYPE_MAGNETIC_FIELD)
        magnetic_read = event.values;
    if (accel_read != null && magnetic_read != null)
    {
        float R[] = new float[9];
```

```
      float I[] = new float[9];
      boolean successsful_read = SensorManager
        .getRotationMatrix(R, I, accel_read,
        magnetic_read);
   if (successsful_read) {
    float orientation[] = new float[3];
    SensorManager.getOrientation(R, orientation);

    azimuth_angle = orientation[0];
     float degrees = ((azimuth_angle * 180f) / 3.14f);
     int degreesInt = Math.round(degrees);

     tv_degrees.setText(Integer.toString(degreesInt)
       + (char) 0x00B0 + " to absolute north.");

     RotateAnimation rotate = new
       RotateAnimation(current_degree, -degreesInt,
       Animation.RELATIVE_TO_SELF, 0.5f,
       Animation.RELATIVE_TO_SELF, 0.5f);
     rotate.setDuration(100);
     rotate.setFillAfter(true);

     iv_compass.startAnimation(rotate);
     current_degree = -degreesInt;
            }
        }
    }
    @Override
    public void onAccuracyChanged(Sensor sensor, int
       accuracy) {
    }
}
```

Code 8.19 (cont'd from the previous page)

8.4. Building and Running the App

If we try to run the app in an emulator, the compass will constantly show the north and the azimuth angle as 0 degrees. We need to try this app on a real device with a magnetometer and accelerometer inside (most Android devices have). Please build the app in Android Studio and install it on a real device. I tried this app on Asus Zenfone and it works as expected:

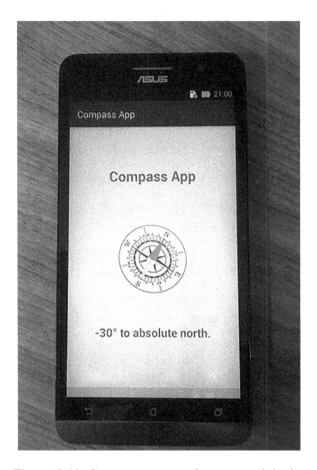

Figure 8.10. Compass app running on a real device

Now, let's take a break and get a strong coffee. In the next chapter, we'll learn using GPS and maps in our app.

ANDRIOD APP # 5: SHOW MY LOCATION: USING GPS AND MAPS

9.1. Creating a Map Project

Geolocation and navigation apps are popular in all mobile platforms. Considering this, most mobile devices especially smartphones include components called GPS receivers. These receivers take microwave band radio signals from global positioning satellites that move in specified orbits around the earth. These GPS signals are extremely weak but thanks to the electronics tech, amplifier and processing circuits in smartphones can utilize these signals for location services.

Anyway, let's start developing our 5th app: Show My Location. In this chapter, you'll learn to use maps and geolocation data from GPS in your apps. It sounds easy but there are some confusing tricks to use the GPS receiver; don't worry I'll show all of them in a while.

In this app, we aim to show our real time location on the map.

Let's start with creating a new Android project and select **Google Maps Activity** as the activity type a shown in Figure 9.1. When we select the Google Maps Activity, the main Java file and the xml layout file of the project are named as MapsActivity.java and activity_maps.xml automatically as in Figure 9.2.

When a Google Maps App project is created, a file named google_maps_api.xml is generated and placed under the res → values folder as shown in Figure 9.3.

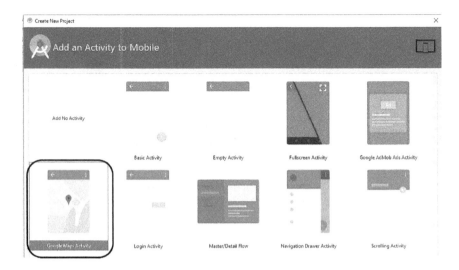

Figure 9.1. Selecting Google Maps Activity during the project creation

Figure 9.2. Filenames automatically assigned by Android Studio

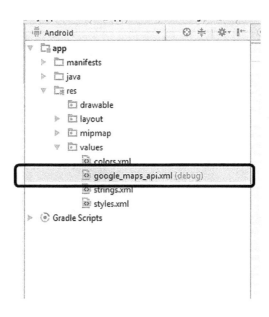

Figure 9.3. google_maps_api.xml file

9.2. Creating and Adding an Api Key

In order to use Google Maps, we need to enter an api (application programming interface) key to the google_maps_api.xml file. The default google_maps_api.xml is as follows:

```
<resources>

<!--
TODO: Before you run your application, you need a
Google Maps API key.

To get one, follow this link, follow the directions
and press "Create" at the end:

https://console.developers.google.com/flows/enableapi
?apiid=maps_android_backend&keyType=CLIENT_SIDE_ANDRO
ID&r=F7:42:43:B5:F0:19:50:79:4E:0E:69:D2:1A:27:3D:7D:
E4:47:EC:6D%3Bcom.example.atomic.myapplication

<string name="google_maps_key"
templateMergeStrategy="preserve"
translatable="false">YOUR_KEY_HERE</string>
</resources>
```
Code 9.1

BEGINNER'S GUIDE TO ANDROID APP DEVELOPMENT

We have to enter the api key to the place indicated by YOUR_KEY_HERE in the file above. So, where should we obtain this key? We just need to go to the website indicated in our google_maps_api.xml file which starts with https://console.developers . When we navigate to this site, we need to select **Create a new project** and hit **Continue** as follows:

Register your application for Google Maps Android API in Google API Console

Google API Console allows you to manage your application and monitor API usage.

Select a project where your application will be registered
You can use one project to manage all of your applications, or you can create a different project for each application.

Create a project ▼

Continue

Figure 9.4. Creating a new project to obtain a new api key for the maps app

In the next dialog, please hit the **Create API Key**:

The API is enabled

The project has been created and Google Maps Android API has been enabled.

Next, you'll need to create an API key in order to call the API.

Create API key

Figure 9.5. Creating the api key

Google console will then display the generated api key as shown below:

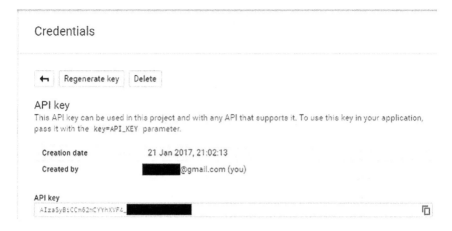

Figure 9.6. The generated api key

Please copy the generated api key and paste it to the place indicated in the google_maps_api.xml file:

Code 9.2

Please note that you need to generate and paste your own key otherwise your app won't work.

9.3. The Default MapsActivity.java File

Let's now view the automatically generated MapsActivity.java file where we'll write the main code:

```
package com.example.atomic.myapplication;

import android.support.v4.app.FragmentActivity;
import android.os.Bundle;

import
com.google.android.gms.maps.CameraUpdateFactory;
import com.google.android.gms.maps.GoogleMap;
import
com.google.android.gms.maps.OnMapReadyCallback;
import
com.google.android.gms.maps.SupportMapFragment;
import com.google.android.gms.maps.model.LatLng;
import
com.google.android.gms.maps.model.MarkerOptions;

public class MapsActivity extends FragmentActivity
implements OnMapReadyCallback {

    private GoogleMap mMap;

    @Override
    protected void onCreate(Bundle
      savedInstanceState) {
      super.onCreate(savedInstanceState);
      setContentView(R.layout.activity_maps);
      // Obtain the SupportMapFragment and get
        notified when the map is ready to be used.
      SupportMapFragment mapFragment =
      (SupportMapFragment) getSupportFragmentManager()
        .findFragmentById(R.id.map);
       mapFragment.getMapAsync(this);
    }


    /**
     * Manipulates the map once available.
     * This callback is triggered when the map is
ready to be used.
     * This is where we can add markers or lines, add
listeners or move the camera. In this case,
     * we just add a marker near Sydney, Australia.
```

```
     * If Google Play services is not installed on
the device, the user will be prompted to install
     * it inside the SupportMapFragment. This method
will only be triggered once the user has
     * installed Google Play services and returned to
the app.
     */
    @Override
public void onMapReady(GoogleMap googleMap) {
  mMap = googleMap;

  // Add a marker in Sydney and move the camera
  LatLng sydney = new LatLng(-34, 151);
  mMap.addMarker(new MarkerOptions().position(sydney)
    .title("Marker in Sydney"));

  mMap.moveCamera(CameraUpdateFactory.newLatLng(sydney)
  );
    }
}
```

Code 9.3 (cont'd from the previous page)

In this code, `mapFragment.getMapAsync(this)` line adds the Map component to the app. Then a `LatLng` object, which holds the latitude and longitude data is created inside the `onMapReady()` method. The code line `LatLng sydney = new LatLng(-34, 151)` declares a `LatLng` object at the latitude and longitude of -34 and 151, which is the coordinates of Sydney, Australia (please note that this point is automatically chosen by Android Studio). Then, a marker on Sydney is placed by the `addMarker()` method which is applied on the map object. And in the last line, the camera is moved to this point by the `moveCamera()` method.

9.4. Running the Maps App for the First Time

We're now ready to try the current state of the app in the emulator. Please hit **Run** in Android Studio and then you should see our app in the emulator as shown in Figure 9.7.

If you see the map with the marker, congratulations. If you cannot see the map, please check the api key section above. Most errors are caused from a wrong api key unless there's another error indicated by the gradle building system.

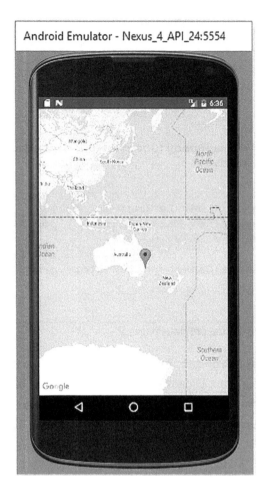

Figure 9.7. Current state of our app

9.5. Implementing the Required Callbacks

We now need to take data from the GPS receiver and then show our current location on the map rather than the default marker. For this, we first implement the required callbacks in the main class definition as follows:

```
public class MapsActivity extends FragmentActivity
implements OnMapReadyCallback, LocationListener,
        GoogleApiClient.ConnectionCallbacks,
GoogleApiClient.OnConnectionFailedListener
        {
```

Code 9.4

In this code snippet, we implemented these additional callbacks: `LocationListener`, `GoogleApiClient.ConnectionCallback` and `GoogleApiClient.OnConnectionFailedListener`. The functions of these callbacks are as follows:

- ➤ `LocationListener`: Activated when the location changes.
- ➤ `GoogleApiClient.ConnectionCallback`: Activated when the device's connection status changes.
- ➤ `GoogleApiClient.OnConnectionFailedListener`: Activated when the connection to the map data server fails.

When we add these callbacks in the class definition in MapsActivity.java, Android Studio gives errors in the callback definition lines. When we click on the red bulb, the option **Implement methods** should be selected as follows:

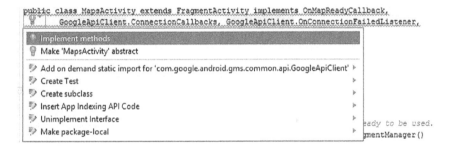

Figure 9.8. Selecting **Implement methods** for correcting the callbacks

The dialog shown in Figure 9.9 appears after choosing to implement methods. Please leave the selected methods and click **OK** in this window. Then, the required methods will be added to MapsActivity.java and the error marks will disappear.

Figure 9.9. Selecting the methods to implement for the callbacks

After implementing these methods, MapsActivity.java looks like follows:

```
package com.example.atomic.myapplication;

import android.location.Location;
import android.location.LocationListener;
import android.support.annotation.NonNull;
import android.support.annotation.Nullable;
import android.support.v4.app.FragmentActivity;
```

```
import android.os.Bundle;

import
com.google.android.gms.common.ConnectionResult;
import
com.google.android.gms.common.api.GoogleApiClient;
import
com.google.android.gms.maps.CameraUpdateFactory;
import com.google.android.gms.maps.GoogleMap;
import
com.google.android.gms.maps.OnMapReadyCallback;
import
com.google.android.gms.maps.SupportMapFragment;
import com.google.android.gms.maps.model.LatLng;
import
com.google.android.gms.maps.model.MarkerOptions;

public class MapsActivity extends FragmentActivity
implements OnMapReadyCallback,
        GoogleApiClient.ConnectionCallbacks,
GoogleApiClient.OnConnectionFailedListener,
        LocationListener{

    private GoogleMap mMap;

    @Override
    protected void onCreate(Bundle
        savedInstanceState) {
    super.onCreate(savedInstanceState);
    setContentView(R.layout.activity_maps);
    // Obtain the SupportMapFragment and get
    notified when the map is ready to be used.
    SupportMapFragment mapFragment =
(SupportMapFragment) getSupportFragmentManager()
        .findFragmentById(R.id.map);
     mapFragment.getMapAsync(this);
    }


    /**
     * Manipulates the map once available.
     * This callback is triggered when the map is
ready to be used.
     * This is where we can add markers or lines,
add listeners or move the camera. In this case,
     * we just add a marker near Sydney, Australia.
     * If Google Play services is not installed on
```

```
the device, the user will be prompted to install
     * it inside the SupportMapFragment. This
method will only be triggered once the user has
     * installed Google Play services and returned
to the app.
     */
@Override
public void onMapReady(GoogleMap googleMap) {
  mMap = googleMap;

// Add a marker in Sydney and move the camera
  LatLng sydney = new LatLng(-34, 151);
  mMap.addMarker(new
    MarkerOptions().position(sydney)
    .title("Marker in Sydney"));
  mMap.moveCamera(CameraUpdateFactory
    .newLatLng(sydney));
    }

    @Override
    public void onLocationChanged(Location
     location) {

    }

    @Override
    public void onStatusChanged(String provider,
     int status, Bundle extras) {

    }

    @Override
    public void onProviderEnabled(String provider)
{

    }

    @Override
    public void onProviderDisabled(String provider)
{

    }

    @Override
    public void onConnected(@Nullable Bundle
     bundle) {
```

```
    }

    @Override
    public void onConnectionSuspended(int i) {

    }

    @Override
    public void onConnectionFailed(@NonNull
       ConnectionResult connectionResult) {

    }
}
```
Code 9.5 (cont'd from the pervious page)

9.6. Populating the Implemented Methods

Let's start populating the implemented methods. First of all, we'll declare the objects those will be used in our code as follows:

```
Location myLastLocation;
LocationRequest myLocationRequest;
GoogleApiClient myGoogleApiClient;
Marker myCurrLocationMarker;
```
Code 9.6

In these declarations, **myLastLocation** holds the location info itself. The remaining objects will be responsible to manage the location request, api related processes and the marker showing the current location, respectively.

The **onCreate()** method contains the jobs to be done when the activity first starts as we learned before. We need to modify it as follows to check the location tracking permission and create a **SupportMapFragment** object that will be used to do things related to the **MapFragment** object of the user interface:

```
protected void onCreate(Bundle savedInstanceState)
{
    super.onCreate(savedInstanceState);
    setContentView(R.layout.activity_maps);

    if (android.os.Build.VERSION.SDK_INT >=
       Build.VERSION_CODES.M) {
```

```
            checkLocationPermission();
    }
    SupportMapFragment mapFragment =
(SupportMapFragment) getSupportFragmentManager()
            .findFragmentById(R.id.map);
    mapFragment.getMapAsync(this);
}
```

Code 9.7 (cont'd from the previous page)

The next method to modify is the onMapReady() method. This method deals with the manipulation of the map once it is available. In this method, the app will check whether the device has Google Play Services installed and if not, the app will prompt to install it. Please remember that map related functions can not run if Google Play Services is not installed. We do these as follows:

```
public void onMapReady(GoogleMap googleMap) {
    mMap = googleMap;
    mMap.setMapType(GoogleMap.MAP_TYPE_NORMAL);

    //Checking Google Play Services version
    if (android.os.Build.VERSION.SDK_INT >=
        Build.VERSION_CODES.M) {
     if (ContextCompat.checkSelfPermission(this,
          Manifest.permission.ACCESS_FINE_LOCATION)
          == PackageManager.PERMISSION_GRANTED)
    {
      buildGoogleApiClient();
      mMap.setMyLocationEnabled(true);
       }
    }
    else {
        buildGoogleApiClient();
        mMap.setMyLocationEnabled(true);
    }
}
```

Code 9.8

The Google api client used in this method is built using the following method:

```
protected synchronized void buildGoogleApiClient()
{
    myGoogleApiClient = new
```

```
GoogleApiClient.Builder(this)
            .addConnectionCallbacks(this)
            .addOnConnectionFailedListener(this)
            .addApi(LocationServices.API)
            .build();
    myGoogleApiClient.connect();
}
```
Code 9.9

When the required permissions are taken and Google api is ready, the app will start tracking the current location inside the onConnected() method as follows:

```
public void onConnected(Bundle bundle) {

  myLocationRequest = new LocationRequest();
  myLocationRequest.setInterval(1000);
  myLocationRequest.setFastestInterval(1000);
  myLocationRequest
    .setPriority(LocationRequest
    .PRIORITY_BALANCED_POWER_ACCURACY);
  if (ContextCompat.checkSelfPermission(this,
    Manifest.permission.ACCESS_FINE_LOCATION)
    == PackageManager.PERMISSION_GRANTED) {
  LocationServices.FusedLocationApi
    .requestLocationUpdates(myGoogleApiClient,
    myLocationRequest, this);
    }

}
```
Code 9.10

In this code, the time intervals are shown in milliseconds. Therefore, the location data is gathered in 1 second intervals. If the intervals get more frequent, the location data will be gathered in shorter intervals but this will drain the battery faster. The setPriority() method is also used to manage the power consumption. In this code, a balanced power usage is selected.

When the location changes, the app will move the marker to the new location. This is done inside the onLocationChanged() method:

```
public void onLocationChanged(Location location) {

    myLastLocation = location;
    if (myCurrLocationMarker != null) {
        myCurrLocationMarker.remove();
    }

    //Move the marker
    LatLng latLng = new
     LatLng(location.getLatitude(),
     location.getLongitude());

    MarkerOptions markerOptions = new
     MarkerOptions();
    markerOptions.position(latLng);
    markerOptions.title("My Position");
    markerOptions.icon(BitmapDescriptorFactory
      .defaultMarker(BitmapDescriptorFactory
      .HUE_MAGENTA));
    myCurrLocationMarker =
        mMap.addMarker(markerOptions);

    //Move the map view
    mMap.moveCamera(CameraUpdateFactory
      .newLatLng(latLng));
    mMap.animateCamera(CameraUpdateFactory
      .zoomTo(11));

    //Stop moving the marker
    if (myGoogleApiClient != null) {
     LocationServices.FusedLocationApi
       .removeLocationUpdates(myGoogleApiClient, this);
    }

}
```

Code 9.11

In this code, getLatitude() and getLongitude() gets the current latitude and longitude and then places them inside the LatLng object. When the location changes, the marker is moved to the new location and the title of the marker is set as **My Position**. Then, the camera is moved to show the current location.

Finally, the permission related `checkLocationPermission()` and `onPermissionRequestResult()` methods are populated as in Code 9.12.

```
public static final int
MY_PERMISSIONS_REQUEST_LOCATION = 99;
public boolean checkLocationPermission(){
    if (ContextCompat.checkSelfPermission(this,
            Manifest.permission.ACCESS_FINE_LOCATION)
            != PackageManager.PERMISSION_GRANTED) {


    if (ActivityCompat.shouldShowRequestPermission
Rationale(this,Manifest.permission.ACCESS_FINE_LOCATI
ON)) {

        ActivityCompat.requestPermissions(this,
            new String[]{Manifest.permission.
            ACCESS_FINE_LOCATION},
            MY_PERMISSIONS_REQUEST_LOCATION);


    } else {

        ActivityCompat.requestPermissions(this,
            new String[]{Manifest.permission.
            ACCESS_FINE_LOCATION},
            MY_PERMISSIONS_REQUEST_LOCATION);
        }
        return false;
    } else {
        return true;
    }
}

@Override
public void onRequestPermissionsResult(int
requestCode,
                                        String
permissions[], int[] grantResults) {
    switch (requestCode) {
        case MY_PERMISSIONS_REQUEST_LOCATION: {

        if (grantResults.length > 0
            && grantResults[0]
                ==PackageManager.PERMISSION_GRANTED) {
```

```
if (ContextCompat.checkSelfPermission(this,
   Manifest.permission.ACCESS_FINE_LOCATION)
   ==PackageManager.PERMISSION_GRANTED) {

   if (myGoogleApiClient == null) {
      buildGoogleApiClient();
      }
      mMap.setMyLocationEnabled(true);
   }
   } else {

   // Toast shows a popup warning on the screen
   Toast.makeText(this, "Permission not given.",
      Toast.LENGTH_LONG).show();
         }
         return;
      }
   }
```

Code 9.12 (cont'd from the previous page)

These methods ask for user permission to track fine location. If the user rejects giving the permission, the message "**Permission not given.**" is shown on the screen as a popup dialog.

The complete MapsActivity.java file is shown in Code 9.13.

```
package com.example.atomic.myapplication;

import android.Manifest;
import android.content.pm.PackageManager;
import android.location.Location;
import android.os.Build;
import android.support.v4.app.ActivityCompat;
import android.support.v4.app.FragmentActivity;
import android.os.Bundle;
import android.support.v4.content.ContextCompat;
import android.widget.Toast;

import com.google.android.gms.common.ConnectionResult;
import com.google.android.gms.common.api.GoogleApiClient;
import com.google.android.gms.location.LocationListener;
import com.google.android.gms.location.LocationRequest;
import com.google.android.gms.location.LocationServices;
import com.google.android.gms.maps.CameraUpdateFactory;
import com.google.android.gms.maps.GoogleMap;
import com.google.android.gms.maps.OnMapReadyCallback;
import com.google.android.gms.maps.SupportMapFragment;
```

```
import
com.google.android.gms.maps.model.BitmapDescriptorFactory;
import com.google.android.gms.maps.model.LatLng;
import com.google.android.gms.maps.model.Marker;
import com.google.android.gms.maps.model.MarkerOptions;

public class MapsActivity extends FragmentActivity
implements OnMapReadyCallback,
        GoogleApiClient.ConnectionCallbacks,
        GoogleApiClient.OnConnectionFailedListener,
        LocationListener {

    private GoogleMap mMap;
    GoogleApiClient myGoogleApiClient;
    Location myLastLocation;
    Marker myCurrLocationMarker;
    LocationRequest myLocationRequest;


    @Override
    protected void onCreate(Bundle savedInstanceState) {
        super.onCreate(savedInstanceState);
        setContentView(R.layout.activity_maps);

        if (android.os.Build.VERSION.SDK_INT >=
            Build.VERSION_CODES.M) {
            checkLocationPermission();
        }
        SupportMapFragment mapFragment =
          (SupportMapFragment) getSupportFragmentManager()
          .findFragmentById(R.id.map);
        mapFragment.getMapAsync(this);
    }


    @Override
    public void onMapReady(GoogleMap googleMap) {
        mMap = googleMap;
        mMap.setMapType(GoogleMap.MAP_TYPE_NORMAL);

        //Initialize Google Play Services
        if (android.os.Build.VERSION.SDK_INT >=
            Build.VERSION_CODES.M) {
            if (ContextCompat.checkSelfPermission(this,
                Manifest.permission.ACCESS_FINE_LOCATION)
                == PackageManager.PERMISSION_GRANTED) {
            buildGoogleApiClient();
            mMap.setMyLocationEnabled(true);
            }
        }
        else {
          buildGoogleApiClient();
          mMap.setMyLocationEnabled(true);
```

```
        }
    }

    protected synchronized void buildGoogleApiClient() {
        myGoogleApiClient = new
            GoogleApiClient.Builder(this)
            .addConnectionCallbacks(this)
            .addOnConnectionFailedListener(this)
            .addApi(LocationServices.API)
            .build();
        myGoogleApiClient.connect();
    }

    @Override
    public void onConnected(Bundle bundle) {

        myLocationRequest = new LocationRequest();
        myLocationRequest.setInterval(1000);
        myLocationRequest.setFastestInterval(1000);
        myLocationRequest.setPriority(LocationRequest
            .PRIORITY_BALANCED_POWER_ACCURACY);
        if (ContextCompat.checkSelfPermission(this,
                Manifest.permission.ACCESS_FINE_LOCATION)
                == PackageManager.PERMISSION_GRANTED) {
        LocationServices.FusedLocationApi
          .requestLocationUpdates(myGoogleApiClient,
           myLocationRequest, this);
        }

    }

    @Override
    public void onConnectionSuspended(int i) {

    }

    @Override
    public void onLocationChanged(Location location) {

        myLastLocation = location;
        if (myCurrLocationMarker != null) {
            myCurrLocationMarker.remove();
        }

        LatLng latLng = new LatLng(location.getLatitude(),
            location.getLongitude());
        MarkerOptions markerOptions = new MarkerOptions();
        markerOptions.position(latLng);
        markerOptions.title("My Position");
        markerOptions.icon(BitmapDescriptorFactory
        .defaultMarker(BitmapDescriptorFactory
        .HUE_MAGENTA));
```

```
myCurrLocationMarker =
   mMap.addMarker(markerOptions);


mMap.moveCamera(CameraUpdateFactory.newLatLng(latLng));

mMap.animateCamera(CameraUpdateFactory.zoomTo(11));

if (myGoogleApiClient != null) {
  LocationServices.FusedLocationApi
    .removeLocationUpdates(myGoogleApiClient, this);
       }

   }

   @Override
public void onConnectionFailed(ConnectionResult
   connectionResult) {

   }

public static final int MY_PERMISSIONS_REQUEST_LOCATION = 99;
    public boolean checkLocationPermission(){
        if (ContextCompat.checkSelfPermission(this,
               Manifest.permission.ACCESS_FINE_LOCATION)
               != PackageManager.PERMISSION_GRANTED) {

        if (ActivityCompat
         .shouldShowRequestPermissionRationale(this,
           Manifest.permission.ACCESS_FINE_LOCATION)) {
           ActivityCompat.requestPermissions(this,
                new String[]{Manifest
                 .permission.ACCESS_FINE_LOCATION},
                 MY_PERMISSIONS_REQUEST_LOCATION);


        } else
         {
           ActivityCompat.requestPermissions(this,
             new String[]{Manifest.permission
             .ACCESS_FINE_LOCATION},
             MY_PERMISSIONS_REQUEST_LOCATION);
             }
           return false;
        } else {
           return true;
        }
    }

   @Override
   public void onRequestPermissionsResult(int
       requestCode,
```

```
    String permissions[], int[] grantResults) {
      switch (requestCode) {
        case MY_PERMISSIONS_REQUEST_LOCATION: {

          if (grantResults.length > 0
              && grantResults[0] ==
              PackageManager.PERMISSION_GRANTED) {


            if (ContextCompat.checkSelfPermission(this,

                Manifest.permission.ACCESS_FINE_LOCATION)
                == PackageManager.PERMISSION_GRANTED) {

              if (myGoogleApiClient == null) {
                buildGoogleApiClient();
                }
             mMap.setMyLocationEnabled(true);
                }


        }
          else {

            Toast.makeText(this, "Permission not given.",
              Toast.LENGTH_LONG).show();
                  }
              return;
              }
          }
       }
    }
```

Code 9.13 (cont'd from the previous page)

Please remember that you can download these files from the book's companion website: www.yamaclis.com/android.

9.7. Adding the Required Permissions to the Manifest File

The AndroidManifest.xml file with the required permissions is also given in Code 9.14.

```
<?xml version="1.0" encoding="utf-8"?>
<manifest
xmlns:android="http://schemas.android.com/apk/res/android"
    package="com.example.atomic.myapplication">

<uses-permission
android:name="android.permission.ACCESS_NETWORK_STATE" />
<uses-permission
```

```
android:name="android.permission.INTERNET" />
<uses-permission
android:name="com.google.android.providers.gsf.permission.
READ_GSERVICES" />
    <!--
        The ACCESS_COARSE/FINE_LOCATION permissions are
not required to use
        Google Maps Android API v2, but you must specify
either coarse or fine
        location permissions for the 'MyLocation'
functionality.
    -->
<uses-permission
android:name="android.permission.ACCESS_COARSE_LOCATION"/>
<uses-permission
android:name="android.permission.ACCESS_FINE_LOCATION" />
<application
 android:allowBackup="true"
 android:icon="@mipmap/ic_launcher"
 android:label="@string/app_name"
 android:supportsRtl="true"
 android:theme="@style/AppTheme">
    <!--
        The API key for Google Maps-based APIs is
defined as a string resource.
        (See the file
"res/values/google_maps_api.xml").
        Note that the API key is linked to the
encryption key used to sign the APK.
        You need a different API key for each
encryption key, including the release key that is used to
        sign the APK for publishing.
        You can define the keys for the debug and
release targets in src/debug/ and src/release/.
    -->
<meta-data
    android:name="com.google.android.geo.API_KEY"
    android:value="@string/google_maps_key"/>

<activity
    android:name=".MapsActivity"
    android:label="@string/title_activity_maps">
    <intent-filter>
    <action android:name="android.intent.action.MAIN"/>

<category
android:name="android.intent.category.LAUNCHER"/>
</intent-filter>
    </activity>
    </application>
</manifest>
```

Code 9.14 (cont'd from the previous page)

The Internet and GPS permissions are added because the map uses both coarse and fine location tracking.

9.8. Running Our App and Sending Custom Coordinates to the Emulator

Please hit the **Run** button in Android Studio to run our Show My Location app. You can run the app in an emulator or on an actual device. The app running in the Nexus 4 emulator is shown in Figure 9.10. If you cannot see the map on your app, most probably it's an error regarding the api key. Please review that section again.

Please note that I have sent custom coordinates to the emulator using its options button as shown in Figure 9.11. The latitude and longitude of the coordinates I've entered are 41.3809 N and 2.11287 E. Can you guess what this famous location is? **Hint:** You can zoom in and out on the emulator's map by double-clicking at a point and then moving the mouse up or down.

It is worth noting that I've tried the app on a real device and it works as expected.

Figure 9.10. Our **Show My Location** app in the emulator

Figure 9.11. Sending custom coordinates to the emulator

Chapter 19

ANDRIOD APP # 6: S.O.S. MESSAGE SENDER

10.1. Introduction

Most of the Android devices have the capability of GSM connection therefore it is useful to learn using SMS messaging in Android. A class called `SmsManager` enables us to design apps that can easily send and receive SMS programmatically. You'll see how this class is used in this chapter.

We'll develop an app which sends the current location to pre-defined recipients using SMS. This app can be useful in case of an emergency in deserts or if you're boozed in a disco when you cannot type text in the message field and need to send your location to a mate to take you home.

10.1. Adding the Required Permissions

Firstly, please create a standard Android Project having an empty activity and a target SDK version of 22 or lower. I named my project as **S.O.S. Sender**. We'll use the location taken from the GPS sensor and send it with SMS. Therefore, we need to add both GPS usage and SMS sending permissions to the **AndroidManifest.xml** file as follows:

```
<uses-permission
android:name="android.permission.ACCESS_FINE_LOCATION
" />
<uses-permission
android:name="android.permission.SEND_SMS" />
```
Code 10.1

After inserting these permissions, **AndroidManifest.xml** file looks as shown below:

```
<?xml version="1.0" encoding="utf-8"?>
```

```
<manifest
xmlns:android="http://schemas.android.com/apk/res/and
roid"
    package="sendsms.example.com.sendsms">

    <uses-permission
android:name="android.permission.ACCESS_FINE_LOCATION
" />
    <uses-permission
android:name="android.permission.SEND_SMS" />

    <application
        android:allowBackup="true"
        android:icon="@mipmap/ic_launcher"
        android:label="@string/app_name"
        android:supportsRtl="true"
        android:theme="@style/AppTheme">
        <activity android:name=".MainActivity">
            <intent-filter>
                <action
android:name="android.intent.action.MAIN" />

                <category
android:name="android.intent.category.LAUNCHER" />
            </intent-filter>
        </activity>
    </application>

</manifest>
```

Code 10.2 (cont'd from the previous page)

10.2. Designing the User Interface

Let's design the user interface now. The user will basically click on an S.O.S. button and nothing else is needed. Therefore, I placed a button widget in the middle the screen in the **activity_main.xml** file as in Figure 10.1 and set its label as **S.O.S.**

The layout_width and layout_height properties of the button are set as wrap_content by default. It means the button's dimensions will just cover the label written on it. However, our button will be used in S.O.S. cases therefore let's enlarge the button to cover the whole user interface. For this, select the button and set its layout_width and layout_height properties as match_parent in Android Studio as shown in Figure 10.2. I've set the button's ID as sendSOS as also shown in this figure.

186

Let's change the button's background colour to red. For this, firstly click the **View all properties** button as indicated by the arrow in Figure 10.3. In the properties list appearing as in Figure 10.4, find the **background** property as indicated in Figure 10.5.

Figure 10.1. The button placed in the middle of the UI

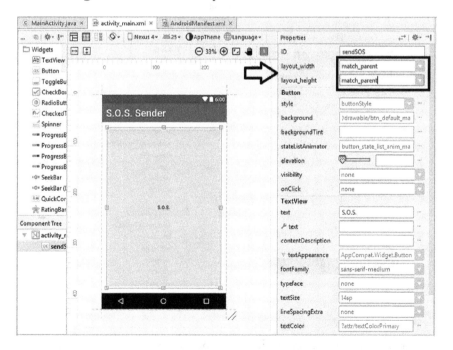

Figure 10.2. Setting the button's dimensions

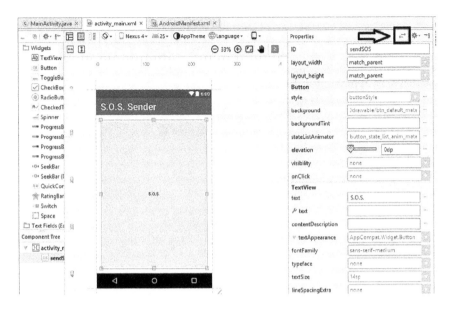

Figure 10.3. Viewing all the properties of the button widget

Figure 10.4. All the properties of the button widget shown in the right pane

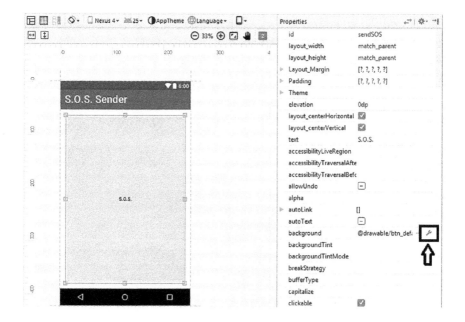

Figure 10.5. Opening the manual editing property of the button

A box in which we can enter the hex colour code of the background will appear as follows:

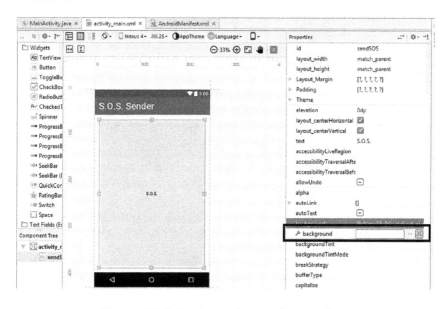

Figure 10.6. Custom colour code entry box

In my opinion, making the S.O.S. button red is a good choice therefore I entered the hex code of red **#FF0000** into this box. However, this is only a personal choice and you can enter any colour code you'd like. You can find the colour codes in several sites such as http://www.color-hex.com/. After entering the colour code, remember to hit **enter** on the keyboard and then the button's colour will be changed to red as follows:

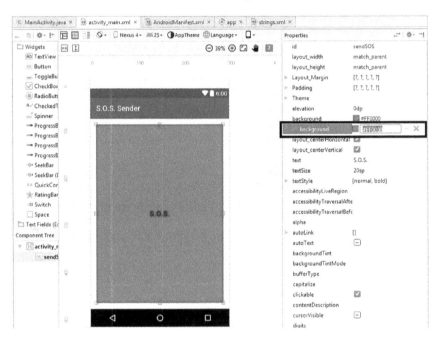

Figure 10.7. Setting the button's background colour

We've set the background colour, great. However the **S.O.S.** label of the button seems tiny now. Let's edit its properties. As the first step, let's switch back to the popular properties of the button by clicking the **View all properties** button again as indicated in Figure 10.8.

I've set the text size as 72sp and its type as bold as shown in Figure 10.9.

10.3. Developing the Main Code

We've now completed the simple UI of our app. Let's move on to the coding part now, which is more fun.

Figure 10.8. Switching back to the common properties

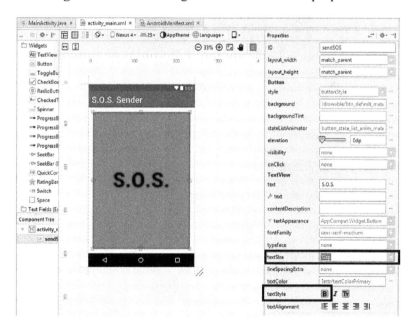

Figure 10.9. Setting the text size and type

The app will take longitude and latitude data from the GPS receiver. This data is a floating point number therefore let's declare two `double` type variables to hold the location data as follows:

```
double latitude = 0;
double longitude = 0;
```
Code 10.3

Let's define a `GPSReceiver` class to manage the GPS part with the `LocationListener` implementation as we did in the previous chapter:

```
public class GPSReceiver implements LocationListener
{
```
Code 10.4

Android Studio will warn us for implementing the required methods at this point:

Figure 10.10. The required methods for the LocationListener

Hit **OK** in this dialog and the methods onLocationChanged(), onStatus(), onProviderEnabled() and onProviderDisabled() will be added to the MainActivity.java. onStatusChanged() is called when a change in the location occurs. Similarly, onProviderEnabled() and onProviderDisabled() methods are called when the GPS receiver is enabled and disabled, respectively. onStatusChanged() is called if the GPS status is changed.

We can populate the onProviderEnabled() and onProviderDisabled() methods as follows:

```
@Override
public void onProviderEnabled(String s) {
    Toast.makeText(getApplicationContext(), "GPS
Enabled!", Toast.LENGTH_LONG).show();

}

@Override
public void onProviderDisabled(String s) {

    Toast.makeText(getApplicationContext(), "Please
enable GPS!", Toast.LENGTH_LONG).show();

}
}
```
Code 10.5

The **Toast** class is used to show a temporary message on the screen. Therefore, if the GPS is disabled, it will display "Please enable GPS!" whereas when the GPS is enabled by the user, it will inform saying that "GPS is enabled!".

The actual location receiving happens inside the onLocationChanged() method. Firstly, let's define a location object which will hold the location data just after the longitude and latitude variable declarations as follows:

```
private LocationManager manager;
```
Code 10.6

Now, we can populate the onLocationChanged() method as follows:

```
public void onLocationChanged(Location location) {
    if (location != null) {
        latitude = location.getLatitude();
        longitude = location.getLongitude();
        Toast.makeText(getApplicationContext(),
"READY TO SEND!!!", Toast.LENGTH_LONG).show();
    }
    else {
        Toast.makeText(getApplicationContext(), "NOT
READY YET...", Toast.LENGTH_LONG).show();
    }
}
```
Code 10.7

If the location data isn't null, i.e. if the location data is received successfully, the longitude and latitude data will be assigned to longitude and latitude variables, respectively. getLongitude() and getLatitude() methods extract the longitude and latitude data from the location object. If the location data is received without any problem, a dialog will display "READY TO SEND!" text on the screen otherwise it'll write "NOT READY YET...".

We've declared our custom method for handling the GPS data operations. Now it's time to define a GPSReceiver object as follows:

```
private GPSReceiver receiver;
```
Code 10.8

We can define it just below the LocationManager object definition shown in Code 10.6 so that it can be accessed from any method in the activity.

Next, let's create the button listener method which will do the SMS sending when the **sendSOS** button's clicked:

```
public void myButtonListenerMethod() {
    Button button = (Button) findViewById(R.id.sendSOS);

    button.setOnClickListener(new View.OnClickListener() {
        @Override
        public void onClick(View v) {
            SmsManager sms = SmsManager.getDefault();
            String phoneNumber = "xxxxxxxxxxxx";
            String messageBody = "Please take me from
```

```
longitude:   " + Double.toString(longitude) + " and
latitude:  " + Double.toString(latitude);
           try {
                sms.sendTextMessage(phoneNumber, null,
messageBody ,null, null);
                Toast.makeText(getApplicationContext(),
"S.O.S. message sent!", Toast.LENGTH_LONG).show();

           } catch (Exception e) {
                Toast.makeText(getApplicationContext(),
"Message sending failed!!!", Toast.LENGTH_LONG).show();
           }
       }
    });
}
```

Code 10.9 (con't from the previous page)

In this button listener method:

➢ The **button** object is created at first,

➢ Then an **SmsManager** object called **sms** is declared inside the **onClick()** method,

➢ Next, the phone number which will receive our SMS is defined in the variable named **phoneNumber** (**please enter a valid receiving phone number in the place of xxxxxxxxx!!!**),

➢ The **messageBody** is also declared as a **String** using the longitude and latitude data.

➢ Finally, the SMS is sent programmatically by the **sendTextMessage()** method.

➢ The try – catch statement is used to check if there's an error sending the SMS message. If there's no error, a message saying "S.O.S. message sent!" will be displayed. Otherwise, it'll display "Message sending failed!!!".

As you can see, the **sendTextMessage()** method has five arguments. We've set the unused arguments to null. We could use these unused arguments for extended functionality such as checking if the SMS is actually received by the receiving part.

Finally, we need to call the button listener and GPS related methods inside the **onCreate()** method as usual:

```
protected void onCreate(Bundle savedInstanceState) {
    super.onCreate(savedInstanceState);
    setContentView(R.layout.activity_main);
    myButtonListenerMethod();
    receiver = new GPSReceiver();
    manager = (LocationManager)
 this.getSystemService(Context.LOCATION_SERVICE);

manager.requestLocationUpdates(LocationManager.GPS_PROVIDE
R, 1000L, 1.0F, receiver);

}
```
Code 10.10

The complete MainActivity.java is also given as follows:

```
package sendsms.example.com.sendsms;

import android.Manifest;
import android.content.Context;
import android.content.pm.PackageManager;
import android.icu.text.DecimalFormat;
import android.location.Location;
import android.location.LocationListener;
import android.location.LocationManager;
import android.os.Build;
import android.support.v4.app.ActivityCompat;
import android.support.v4.content.ContextCompat;
import android.support.v7.app.AppCompatActivity;
import android.os.Bundle;
import android.telephony.SmsManager;
import android.view.View;
import android.widget.Button;
import android.widget.EditText;
import android.widget.TextView;
import android.widget.Toast;

import java.util.function.DoubleUnaryOperator;

public class MainActivity extends AppCompatActivity {

    private LocationManager manager;
    private GPSReceiver receiver;
    double latitude = 0;
    double longitude = 0;

    @Override
    protected void onCreate(Bundle
```

```
savedInstanceState) {
        super.onCreate(savedInstanceState);
        setContentView(R.layout.activity_main);
        myButtonListenerMethod();
        receiver = new GPSReceiver();
        manager = (LocationManager)
this.getSystemService(Context.LOCATION_SERVICE);

manager.requestLocationUpdates(LocationManager.GPS_PR
OVIDER, 1000L, 1.0F, receiver);


    }

    public void myButtonListenerMethod() {
        Button button = (Button)
findViewById(R.id.sendSOS);

        button.setOnClickListener(new
View.OnClickListener() {
                @Override
                public void onClick(View v) {
                    SmsManager sms =
SmsManager.getDefault();
                    String phoneNumber = "05363624223";
                    String messageBody = "Please take me
from longitude:  " + Double.toString(longitude) + "
and latitude: " + Double.toString(latitude);
                    try {
                        sms.sendTextMessage(phoneNumber,
null, messageBody ,null, null);

Toast.makeText(getApplicationContext(), "S.O.S.
message sent!", Toast.LENGTH_LONG).show();

                    } catch (Exception e) {

Toast.makeText(getApplicationContext(), "Message
sending failed!!!", Toast.LENGTH_LONG).show();
                    }
                }
        });
    }
    public class GPSReceiver implements
LocationListener {
    @Override
    public void onLocationChanged(Location location)
{
```

```
        if (location != null) {
            latitude = location.getLatitude();
            longitude = location.getLongitude();
            Toast.makeText(getApplicationContext(),
"READY TO SEND!!!", Toast.LENGTH_LONG).show();
        }
        else {
            Toast.makeText(getApplicationContext(),
"NOT READY YET...", Toast.LENGTH_LONG).show();
        }

    }

    @Override
    public void onStatusChanged(String s, int i,
Bundle bundle) {

    }

    @Override
    public void onProviderEnabled(String s) {
        Toast.makeText(getApplicationContext(), "GPS
Enabled!", Toast.LENGTH_LONG).show();

    }

    @Override
    public void onProviderDisabled(String s) {

        Toast.makeText(getApplicationContext(),
"Please enable GPS!", Toast.LENGTH_LONG).show();

    }
    }
}
```

Code 10.11 (cont'd from the previous pages)

10.4. Building and Running the App

Since this app uses SMS functionality, it needs a GSM connection therefore it cannot be simulated in an emulator. Please connect a real Android device to your computer and select it for running this app after hitting the **Run** button in Android Studio as follows:

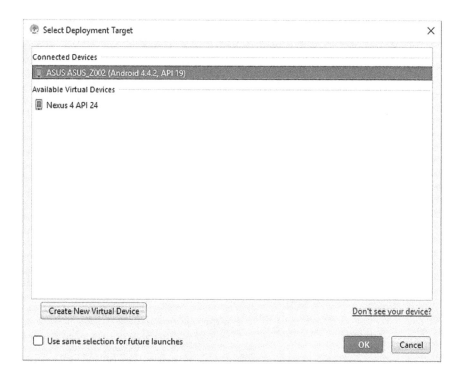

Figure 10.11. Selecting a real Android device with GSM functionality

When the app starts, please wait a moment to see the **READY TO SEND!** message on the screen and then if you click on the giant **S.O.S.** button, the phone will send your current location to the hardcoded phone number. In the receiving phone, you'll see a text such as **Please take me from longitude: -1.985401 and latitude 52.397618**. The coordinates will obviously be different depending on your location.

It is again worth noting that you can download the complete project files, images, etc. from the book's companion website: www.yamaclis.com/android.

ANDRIOD APP # 7: DEVELOPING A 2D PLATFORM GAME IN UNITY FOR ANDROID

Games are among the most popular apps. Game developers earn good money once the gamers get addicted to their games. However, developing a game is not a simple task since a good game should have an exciting story, good graphics, realistic physics rules and efficient code to glue all these together. Fortunately, game development frameworks make this task easier. There are many game development tools using various programming languages. Unity is one of the most popular game development tools. Unity lets us to develop both 2-dimensional (2D) and 3-dimensional (3D) games. We will develop a simple 2D platform game using Unity for Android in this chapter.

The name of the game we will develop is **Random Platformer**. The idea is simple: the main character will walk on platforms. He will try to collect **yellow coins** and avoid **red monsters** while he's trying to complete the level. When he collects a coin, the item will disappear and **the score will increase by a random number between 0 and 5**. When the user accidentally touches a monster, the score will **decrease by a number between 0 and 10**. As you may have guessed, we will use our the `Random` class to generate these random score increments or decrements. When the character falls down the platform, the level will restart with the score reset.

It is worth noting that we also will define the touch controls for the control of the main character in the code while we are implementing the game logic.

11.1. Downloading and Installing Unity

First of all, we need to download and install the Unity. For this, please navigate to their official website at https://store.unity.com. You'll be presented by the following options:

Figure 11.1. Unity download options

Since we are a beginner, it is OK to select the personal edition. Therefore, click the Try Personal link to navigate to the following page:

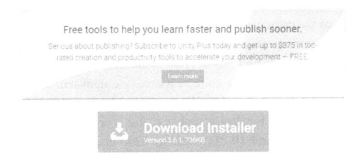

Figure 11.2. The download page for the installer

Click the Download Installer link to download the small program that will manage the installation. The executable file named UnityDownloadAssistant-5.6.1f1.exe will be downloaded (note that the filename might have been changed as you read this). Click on this executable file once it is downloaded on your computer. The Download Assistant will be launched:

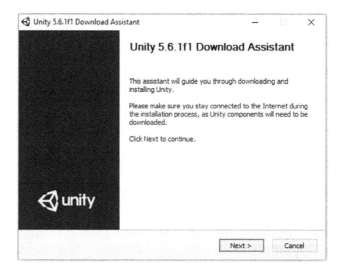

Figure 11.3. Unity download assistant

When you click Next, the installer will connect to their server and the up-to-date License Agreement will be displayed. If you accept the terms of the agreement, check the corresponding box and click Next:

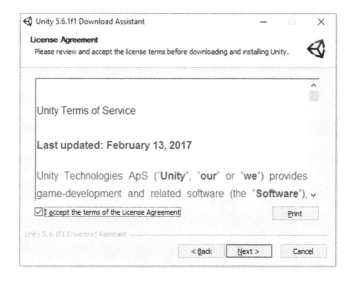

Figure 11.4. The License Agreement window

Select the 64-bit option and click Next:

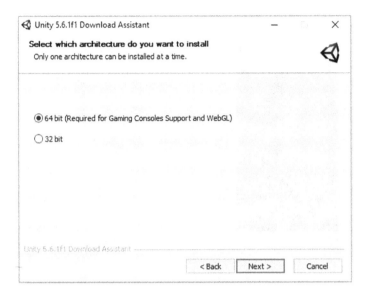

Figure 11.5. The architecture selection dialog

The download options will be shown:

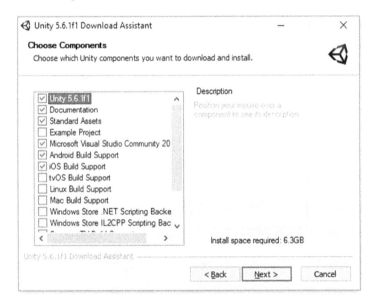

Figure 11.6. The component selection dialog

There are many download options as you can see from the list. I have selected the checked components which are enough for Android game development. You can of course install support for mobile platforms if you'd like to install your games on phones or tablets. Installer shows the download amount as 2.5GB for which you may have to wait a while depending on your connection speed. Click Next to check select the installation path:

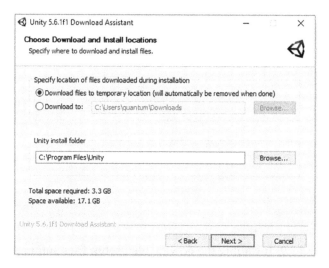

Figure 11.7. Selecting the installation path

The installation assistant will download the setup after clicking Next:

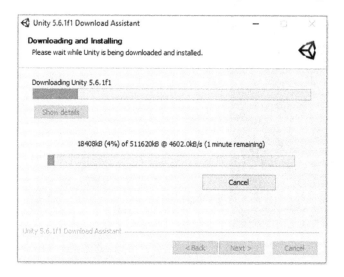

Figure 11.8. Installation assistant downloading the setup files

After the download is complete, the installation assistant will automatically install the program:

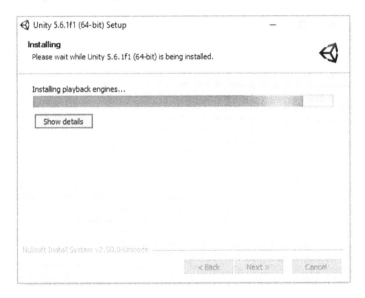

Figure 11.9. Installing the downloaded setup files automatically

Finally, the installation will be completed and we can launch Unity:

Figure 11.10. Installation complete dialog

11.2. Creating the Game Project

When we launch Unity for the first time, it will display a welcome dialog and ask us to sign in. We can work offline however in order to download the resources provided by Unity, we need to sign in. If you don't have a Unity account, click the **create one** link, creating a personal account is free:

Figure 11.11. The welcome screen

After you create your account and sign in, the following window will appear:

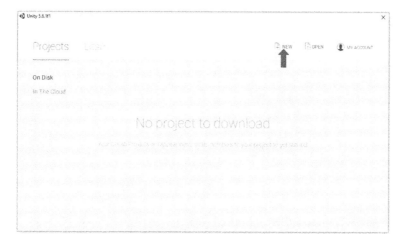

Figure 11.12. The create/open project dialog

Click the **New** button as indicated by the arrow and the dialog for editing the details of the new project will be shown:

Figure 11.13. The details window

I named the project as **Random Platformer** and selected 2D:

Figure 11.14. The project details and type

Click the **Create project** button. The Unity will then create and open the project as follows:

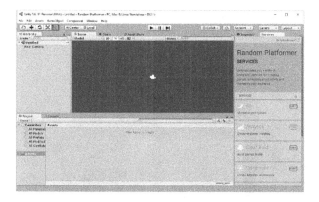

Figure 11.15. The main Unity window

⚠️ It is highly recommended to download the colour Figures of this chapter from the book's website www.yamaclis.com/android and follow this chapter with those Figures. It is because B&W Figures on the printed version are not easy to follow; some objects cannot be seen at all. Sorry about this but had to print this book in B&W for providing it with a decent price tag.

11.3. Adding Assets to the Project

Unity provides ready-made assets for use in our games. We can use them or create our own assets. For our platform game, it is better to add the provided free 2D assets and then manipulate them per our need. For this, click Assets → Import Package → 2D as shown below:

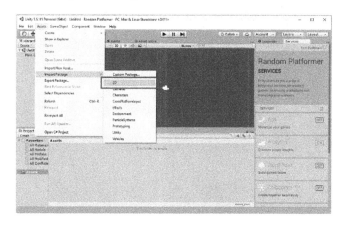

Figure 11.16. Importing 2D assets

A dialog to select the assets for importing will be displayed. All assets are selected by default. Click **Import** button to import these assets to our project:

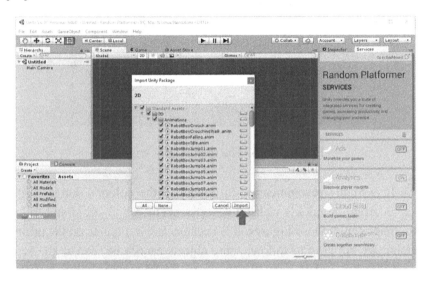

Figure 11.17. Importing all 2D assets

Imported assets will be placed in the **Standard Assets** folder and shown in the project browser:

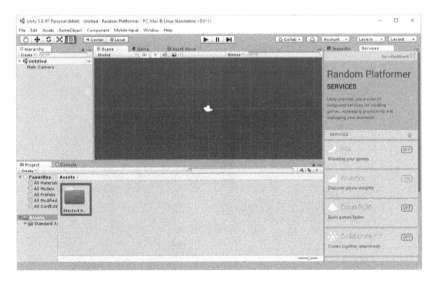

Figure 11.18. Assets in the Standard Assets folder

Let's overview the sections of the main window as below:

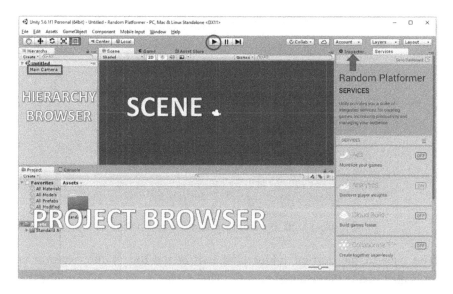

Figure 11.19. The main window of Unity

- We design the game scene in the section marked by Scene.
- We add/view the assets and game code of the project from the Project Browser.
- The components of the game are shown in the Hierarchy Browser. When a project is created, the component called Main Camera (as shown inside the rectangle) is automatically added.
- We can test our game by clicking the Start button indicated inside the circle. We can stop the game by clicking the same button.
- Finally, we can view/change the properties of game components from the Inspector pane shown by the arrow.

We can view the assets by double-clicking the Standard Assets folder just as in the usual Windows Explorer. There are four folders: 2D, CrossPlatform, Editor and Utility. These folders also have other folders inside in a logical hierarchy. Navigate to Assets → Standard Assets → 2D → Prefabs in the Project Explorer as follows:

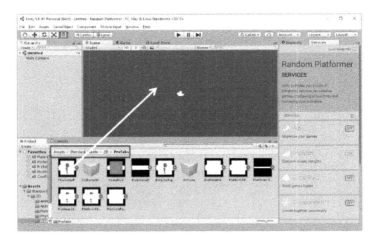

Figure 11.20. Navigating to the Prefabs folder

The path to the current folder is shown at the top of the explorer as indicated inside the rectangle above. This folder contains 2D prefabs (i.e. templates) that we can modify and use in our game.

We need a character in our game and let's use the one provided by the Standard Assets. Drag and drop the CharacterRobotBoy from Prefabs to the scene as shown by the arrow in Figure 11.20. Then, the RobotBoy will be shown in the scene:

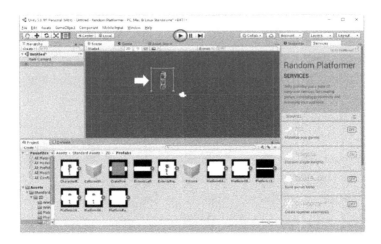

Figure 11.21. RobotBoy character in the scene

We can test the project by clicking the Play button that is indicated inside the circle. The Game view will appear and our character will quickly fall out of the view:

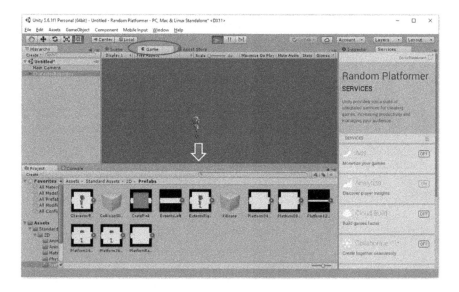

Figure 11.22. The game view

When we click the Play button, our project is built and the Game view (the tab shown inside the ellipse) is displayed instead in the middle pane. By default, gravity is applied on our character therefore he immediately falls down. This is because this character from the Standard Assets is defined as a **RigidBody 2D** which has the **Gravity Scale** of 3 by default. We can view and change this by selecting the character and opening the **Inspector** tab at the right pane as shown in Figure 11.23.

We can view/change all of the properties of game objects from the Inspector. For example, if we change the Gravity Scale of the RobotBoy as 0, then it will just stay at its place when we run the game again as shown in Figures 11.24 and 11.25, respectively.

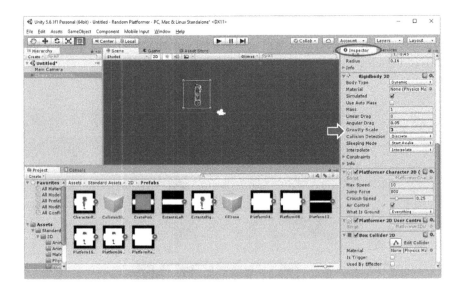

Figure 11.23. The default parameters of the RobotBoy character

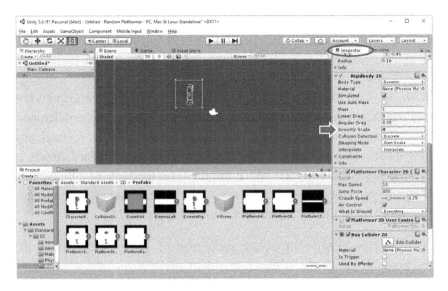

Figure 11.24. The Gravity Scale of the RobotBoy changed as 0

- Note that the changed parameter is indicated by bold in the Inspector.

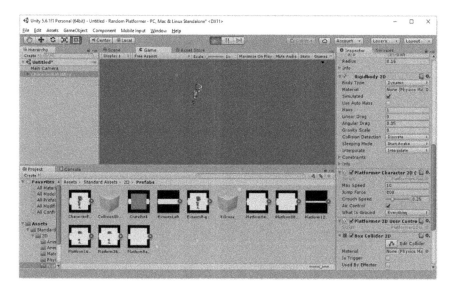

Figure 11.25. Our character hanging in the air with a Gravity Scale of 0

Let's restore the Gravity Scale to its default value, 3, since we are developing a platform game in which the character will have to advance on platforms and has the fall down if he cannot jump properly.

Now, place a Platform04x01 just below the character as shown below:

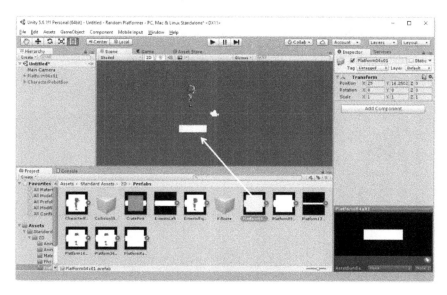

Figure 11.26. Placing a Platform below the character

The platforms in the Standard Assets folder have the Box Collider 2D properties by default. This makes them interact and hold rigid bodies. You can see this property by selecting the Collider part of the platform from the hierarchy and viewing its properties from the Inspector:

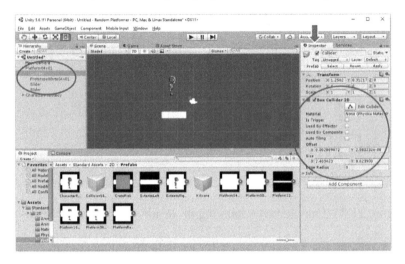

Figure 11.27. Viewing the Collider property of the Platform

Build and run the project again and you will see that our character will fall on the platform stand on it:

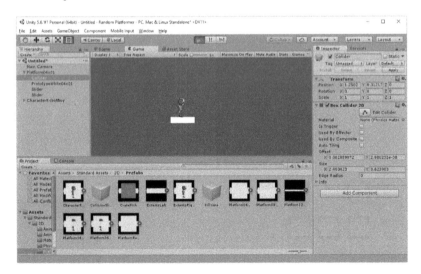

Figure 11.28. Our character standing on the platform

We can move the character to left and right using the left and right arrow keys on the keyboard. Moreover, he can jump and crouch by the space bar and the Ctrl key.

When our character falls down the platform, he will disappear and nothing will happen because we haven't defined anything to detect his falls yet.

Now, stop the test mode by clicking the Play button to switch back to the Scene view. In the Scene view:

• We can zoom in and out by mouse scrolls and
• We can shift the scene by the left mouse key when holding the Alt button on the keyboard.

We have only used the imported 2D assets. Now, let's import our own image files to be used as sprites in the game. There are two images you can download from the book's website for this. One of them is the yellow coin and the other is the red monster image (yellowCoin.png and redMonster.png files). After you download them on your computer, drag and drop them to the Unity window into the project explorer (Assets → Standard Assets →2D → Prefabs folder):

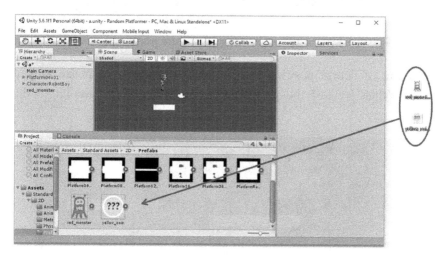

Figure 11.29. Adding image files to our project

We now have our main character, platform, yellow coin and red monster sprites and ready to design our level visually and write the required game code in Unity. It is worth noting that we will use C# (pronounced as c sharp) programming language for coding in Unity, which is very similar to Java we used in the previous chapters. We'll design a sample short level here to see how to develop a game project but after you grasp these basics, you can design your own complete level and game bounded only with your imagination.

First of all, let's use the platform template to place various platforms to our scene. We can just copy-paste the platform we placed in our scene. Our RobotBoy will walk on these platforms and will have to jump when there is a gap between them:

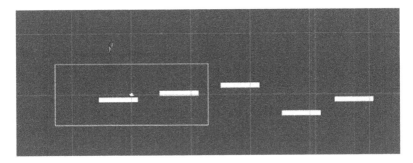

Figure 11.30. Positioning of the platforms

You can of course position the platforms differently or resize as you wish. When we test the project now, we will a scene similar to the following:

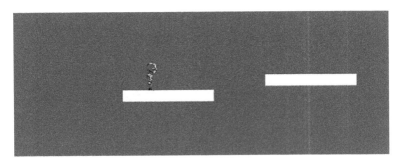

Figure 11.31. Testing the scene

We can move our RobotBoy using the left-right arrows and jump by the space key. However, when we jump from the second platform to the right, RobotBoy will go right but we will no longer be able to see him:

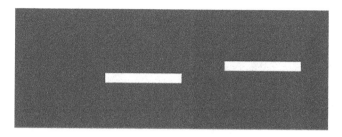

Figure 11.32. Main character disappeared from the camera view

This is because our main camera is not set up for following our character. We need to add a script to our project for this. Please navigate to Assets → Standard Assets → 2D → Scripts in the project explorer. Then drag and drop the first script named **Camera2Dfollow.cs** to the **Main Camera** object in the hierarchy view:

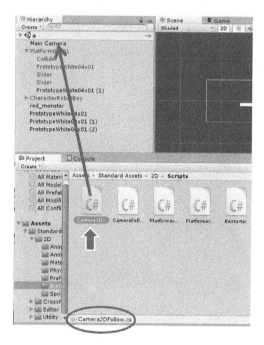

Figure 11.33. Adding the script required for the Main Camera

Now, select Main Camera from the hierarchy and find its properties from the Inspector, we will see a newly added section called **Camera 2D Follow (Script)**:

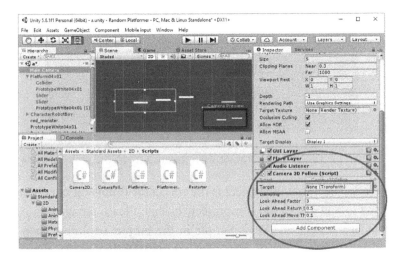

Figure 11.34. The newly added 2D Follow script in the inspector

There is a **Target** section as indicated inside the rectangle. That variable is the target of the camera, which will be the RobotBoy for this project. In order to set it as the RobotBoy, drag and drop **CharacterRobotBoy from the hierarchy** to the **Target box**:

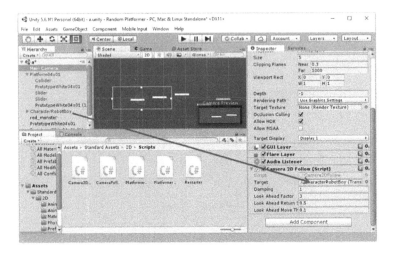

Figure 11.35. Setting the camera target

The Target box will read CharacterRobotBoy (Transform) after this operation. If we test the game now, we will see that the Main Camera follows our character as it advances to the right:

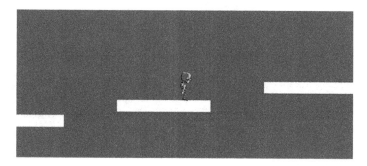

Figure 11.36. Camera follows our character

Great, now it is time to place the red monsters and the yellow coins. As we did for the character and the platform, we will drag and drop red_monster and yellow_coin objects from the Prefabs folder to the scene. Let's place one red_monster and one yellow_coin to set their properties. We will copy-paste them once their properties are set. I placed a red_monster and a yellow_coin by the drag&drop operation as follows:

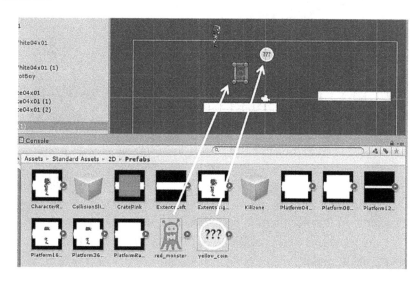

Figure 11.37. Adding the red_monster and yellow_coin to the scene

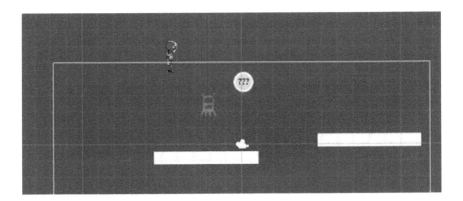

Figure 11.38. Red monster and yellow coin added to the scene

When we test the game now, we will see that the red monster and the yellow coin will just stay at their places:

Figure 11.39. Red monster and yellow coin staying at their positions

It will be better to add some action to the red monster and the yellow coin. For example, we can make them to fall on the platform and bounce back. Let's do this for the red_monster first. Select the red_monster and click Component → Physics 2D → Rigidbody 2D to add the rigid body property to this asset:

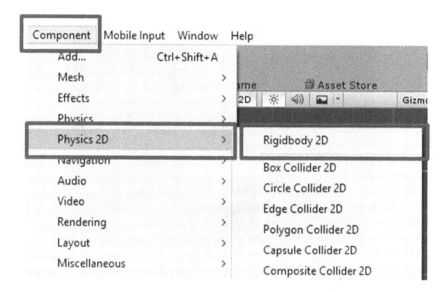

Figure 11.40. Adding the Rigidbody 2D property

Then, select Component → Physics 2D → Box Collider 2D to make it collide with the platform:

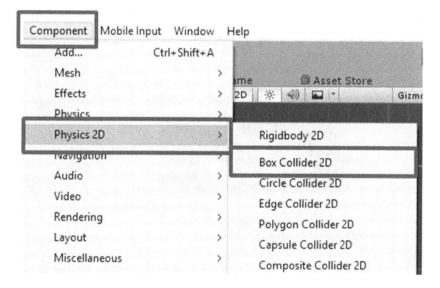

Figure 11.41. Adding the collision property to the red_monster

When we test the game now, we will see that the red_monster will fall on the platform and stay there:

Figure 11.42. The red_monster staying on the platform (please refer to the colour figure online as the monster cannot be seen in B&W printed book)

We want the monster to bounce off the platform. We will add the BouncyBox material as the Collider material for the monster. For this, navigate to Assets → Standard Assets → 2D → PhysicsMaterials in the project explorer and drag&drop it as the Material of Box Collider 2D property of the monster:

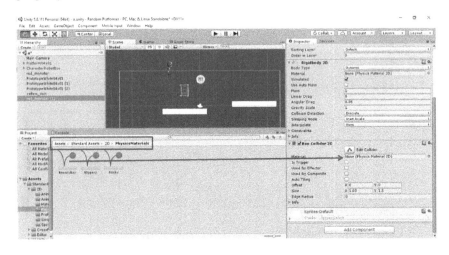

Figure 11.43. Adding the BouncyBox to the monster's Collider property

The Material will then be set as the BouncyBox:

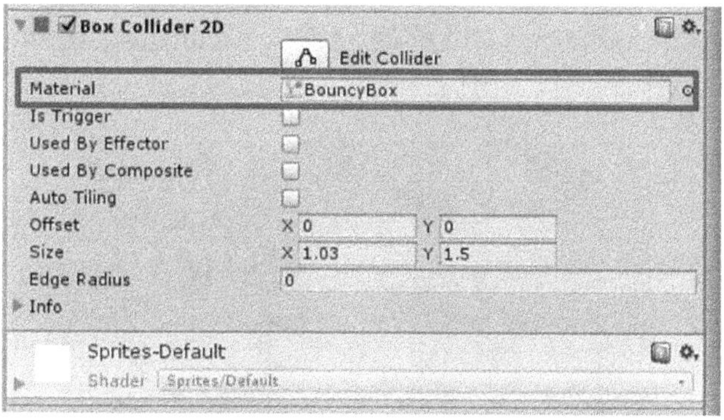

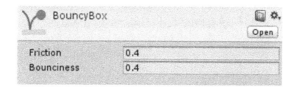

Figure 11.44. The Material of the red monster set as BouncyBox

When we run our game now, the red monster will bounce off the platform three times and then stay on the platform. This is because it loses its kinetic energy due to the default Friction and Bounciness values of the BouncyBox material. In order to bounce the monster indefinitely, we will set these values. Please double-click on the BouncyBox text shown inside the rectangle in Figure 11.44 to open the properties of the BouncyBox material:

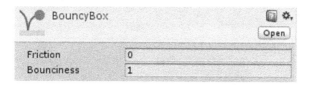

Figure 11.45. Default parameters of the BouncyBox

Please set the values of the Friction and Bounciness as 0 and 1, respectively. These values will let the monster to bounce without losing any energy therefore bouncing indefinitely:

Figure 11.46. New values of the parameters of the BouncyBox material

When we run the game now, we will see that the red monster bounces continuously. Please apply these steps (starting from page 404) also for the yellow coin. Then, we will have a bouncing monster and a coin in our scene:

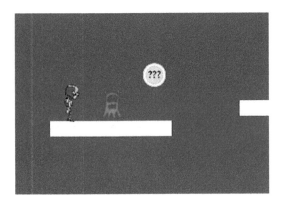

Figure 11.47. Red monster and yellow coin bouncing in the scene

Since we placed them at different heights in the beginning, their movement will be asynchronous therefore adding sort of difficulty to our simple game.

On the other hand, we need to set tags for these objects to access them in our C# code. For this select the red monster in the scene and find the Add Tag section in the Inspector menu:

Figure 11.48. Adding a new Tag

Find and click the plus sign (+) as shown below:

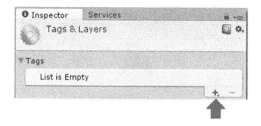

Figure 11.49. Adding a new tag

Set the new tag as **red_monster** and click the Save button:

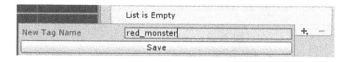

Figure 11.50. Setting the name of the new tag

Add another new tag again by clicking the plus button and set its name as **yellow_coin**:

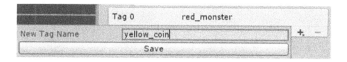

Figure 11.51. Setting another tag for the yellow_coin

Don't forget to click the Save button.

Now select the red_monster again in the scene and set its tag as red_monster from the Inspector pane:

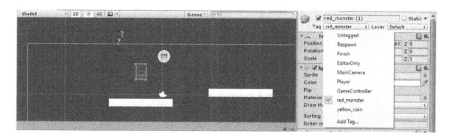

Figure 11.52. Setting the tag for the red_monster

Now, select the yellow coin and similarly set its tag as yellow_coin:

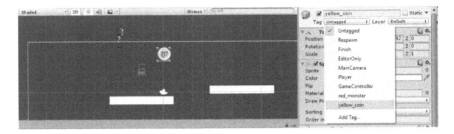

Figure 11.53. Setting the tag of the yellow coin

We now have set the properties of the red monster and yellow coin. Now, copy and paste them a few times wherever you want them in the scene. I placed them as follows:

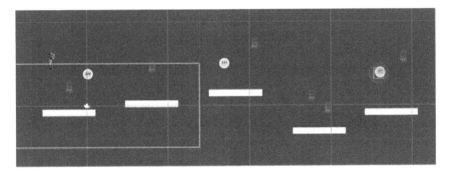

Figure 11.54. Layout of the scene

When we test our game now, we will see that the monsters and coins are bouncing and when our RobotBoy touches them, they are affected by the applied force and move accordingly.

Finally, let's add two sprites: one at the bottom of the scene and the other at the end of the level. The bottom sprite will be used to check if the RobotBoy fell off the platforms. When the RobotBoy touches this sprite, it will mean that the character fell and the level will restart. Similarly, if the character touches the sprite at the end of the level, this will mean that the player finished the level successfully and a big text displaying **Level complete!** will appear.

We will create a new square sprite for forming the ground sprite. For this, click the Create button just below the Project tab:

Figure 11.55. The Create menu

Then, select Sprites → Square from the Create menu:

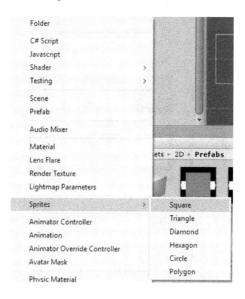

Figure 11.56. Creating a square sprite

The new square sprite will be added to the current project folder. Rename it as **ground** as shown in Figure 11.57. Then, drag&drop it to the scene below the platforms as in Figure 11.58.

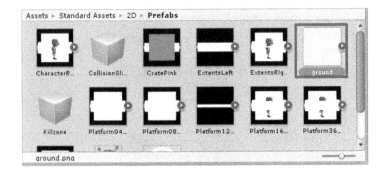

Figure 11.57. The newly added sprite renamed as **ground**

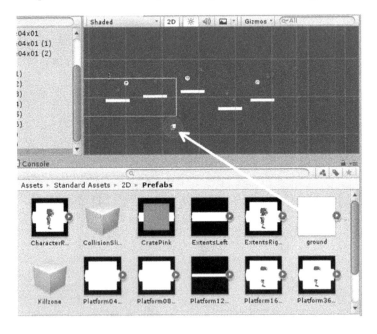

Figure 11.58. Adding the ground sprite to the scene

Now, extend the ground sprite by dragging its edges so that it covers the bottom of the scene as shown inside the rectangle in Figure 11.59.

We will now add a tag to the ground sprite. Select the ground sprite if it is not already selected and find the Tag menu from the Inspector as we did on page 226. Add a new tag named ground and then set the tag of the ground sprite as ground as shown in Figure 11.60. Remember that we need tags to access these objects from the C# code.

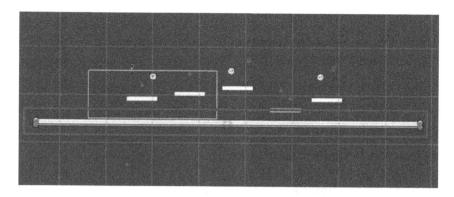

Figure 11.59. The ground sprite spanning the bottom of the scene

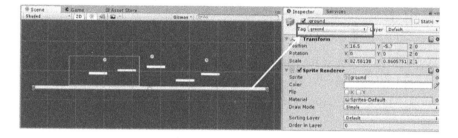

Figure 11.60. Setting the tag of the ground sprite

Now, add the Box Collider 2D to ground:

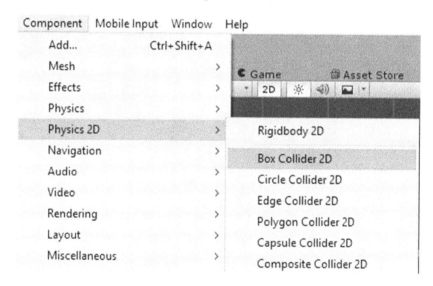

Figure 11.61. Adding the Box Collider 2D property to the ground

The ground sprite appears as white by default. Let's change its colour as red to differentiate from normal platforms. We can change its colour from the Sprite Renderer section of the Inspector pane. Click the Color property to open the colour selection dialog:

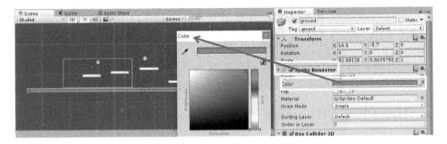

Figure 11.62. Setting the colour of the ground as red

We will now place the finish sprite (finish flag). When the RobotBoy touches this sprite, the level will be completed. Create a square sprite as we did for the ground and name it as **finish**. Place it at the end of the scene:

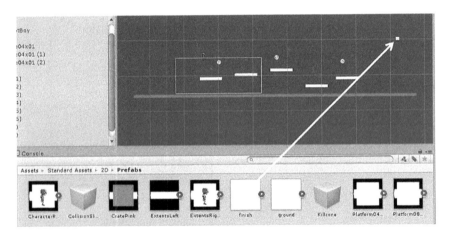

Figure 11.63. Adding the finish sprite

Make it longer by dragging its edges and set its colour as green:

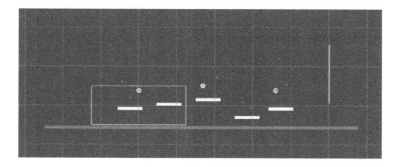

Figure 11.64. The finish sprite made longer and its colour set as green

Finally, add a new tag named **finish** in the Inspector as we did before, and set the tag of the finish sprite as **finish**:

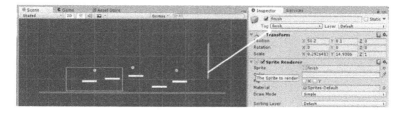

Figure 11.65. Setting the tag of the finish sprite

Don't forget to add the Box Collider 2D property to the finish sprite to be able to make our RobotBoy to collide with it.

We can now test the visual interface of our simple platformer. When our RobotBoy hits the red monsters or yellow coins, they will scatter around in a funny way. However, our aim will be to avoid the monsters and collect the coins. When the RobotBoy touches a monster, the monster will disappear and the score will randomly decrease. Similarly, when he collects a coin, the coin will disappear and the score will randomly increase. Furthermore, when the RobotBoy falls on the red ground, the level will restart. We will use our C# skills to implement this logic.

11.4. Using C# to Implement Game Logic

We will use C# in Unity to implement the game logic. Fortunately, Unity provides various useful classes and methods to do this. When we consider the aim and logic of our game, it is easy to see that the gameplay will be in fact based on touches (collisions):

- If our main character, the RobotBoy, **collides with a monster**, the score will decrease and the monster will disappear,
- If the RobotBoy **collides with a coin**, the score will increase and the coin will disappear,
- If the RobotBoy **collides with the red ground sprite**, the level will restart and,
- If the RobotBoy **collides with the green finish sprite**, the level will be completed.

As you may have guessed, we will utilize several conditional statements (if-else or switch-case structures) to check these collisions.

We will now create a new C# file in our project and write the necessary collision detection code inside this file. For this, click the **Create** button in the project pane:

Figure 11.66. Create button in the project pane

Then, select **C# Script** from the menu:

Figure 11.67. Creating a new C# script

Name the new C# file as GameScript:

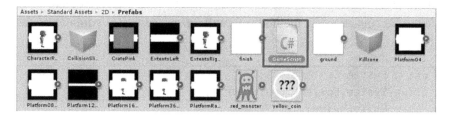

Figure 11.68. The new C# file named as GameScript

Now, open this C# file by double-clicking in the project explorer. You'll see that it is opened in Visual Studio:

```
GameScript.cs ✱ ×
Random Platformer.Plugins                    GameScript                    Start()
  1    using System.Collections;
  2    using System.Collections.Generic;
  3    using UnityEngine;
  4
  5    public class GameScript : MonoBehaviour {
  6
  7        // Use this for initialization
  8        void Start () {
  9
 10        }
 11
 12        // Update is called once per frame
 13        void Update () {
 14
 15        }
 16    }
 17
```

Figure 11.69. GameScript.cs opened in Visual Studio

Note that we will not build the project in Visual Studio; we will utilize Visual Studio as an editor to write and manage the C# code. The game project will be built in Unity.

As it can be seen from the figure above, GameScript.cs file includes two methods by default: Start() and Update(). We can write the code regarding the initialization and update actions inside these methods when needed.

There are special methods in Unity used for the implementation of the game mechanism. One of these methods is the OnCollisionEnter2D method which is automatically called when a collision occurs during the gameplay. Let's now implement this method below the Update() method. When we let Visual Studio to autocomplete the OnCollisionEnter2D method it will also add its parameters as (Collision2D **collision**):

```
using System.Collections;
using System.Collections.Generic;
using UnityEngine;

public class GameScript : MonoBehaviour {

    // Use this for initialization
    void Start () {

    }

    // Update is called once per frame
    void Update () {

    }

    void OnCollisionEnter2D(Collision2D collision)
    {
        // Collision code will be written here

    }
}
```

Code 11.1

We need to declare a variable to hold the score. We can place this declaration just before our new method to make it accessible from other methods when needed:

```
using System.Collections;
using System.Collections.Generic;
using UnityEngine;

public class GameScript : MonoBehaviour {

  // Use this for initialization
```

```
void Start () {
}

// Update is called once per frame
void Update () {

}

    int score = 0;
    void OnCollisionEnter2D(Collision2D collision)
    {
      // Collision code will be written here

    }
}
```

Code 11.2 (cont'd)

We are now ready to write the collision code. As we have stated before, the method OnCollisionEnter2D will be called each time a collision occurs. Therefore we need to check which characters are involved in the collision. We do this by extracting the tag of the colliding object:

```
string objectTag = collision.collider.gameObject.tag;
```

Code 11.3

We will now use if-else statements to check the obtained tag against the tags of the objects we set before. Firstly, if the colliding object is a yellow coin, we will increase the score by a random amount between 1 and 5:

```
if (objectTag == "yellow_coin")
{
  int randomIncrement = UnityEngine.Random.Range(1, 5);
  score = score + randomIncrement;
  print(score);
  Destroy(collision.collider.gameObject);
}
```

Code 11.4

An integer named `randomIncrement` is created and given a random value between 1 and 5 using the random number generation method of the UnityEngine class by the code line `UnityEngine.Random.Range(1, 5);`. Then, this random number is added to the score. In the next line, the score is printed in the console of the Unity using the `print` method. Finally, the coin is destroyed by the code line `Destroy(collision.collider.gameObject);`.

Please save the GameScript.cs file in Visual Studio and switch to Unity. We need to attach this script to our RobotBoy so that its collisions will be checked. For this, drag&drop the GameScript.cs from the project explorer to CharacterRobotBoy in the hierarchy pane:

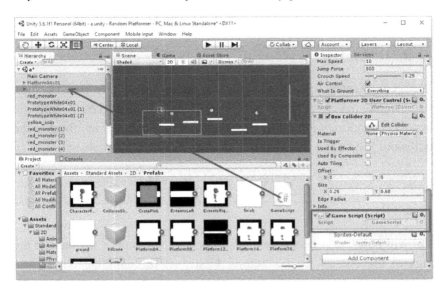

Figure 11.70. Attaching the GameScript.cs to the RobotBoy

We are now ready to test our code. Firstly, click the Console tab which is next to the Create button in the project pane to open the Console. We will see the updated score as we collect the coins in the Console window with the `print(score)` code line:

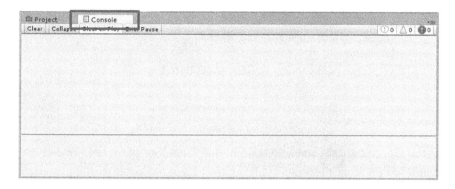

Figure 11.71. Opening the Console in Unity

Now, click the Play button in Unity to start testing our game at this stage. As you collect the coins, you'll see that the score shown in the Console window will increment and the collected coin will disappear:

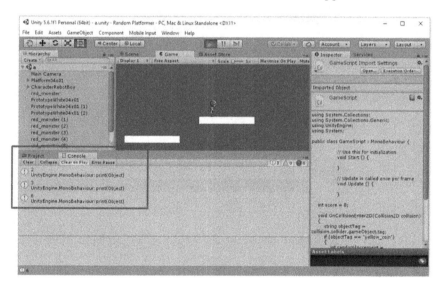

Figure 11.72. Score increases randomly as the RobotBoy collects coins

Similarly, we will decrease the score when the RobotBoy collides with a red monster. We will check the tag to see if it is red_monster and the score will decrease randomly by a number in the range of 1 and 10:

```
if (objectTag == "red_monster")
{
```

```
        int randomDecrement = UnityEngine.Random.Range(1, 10);
        score = score - randomDecrement;
        print(score);
        Destroy(collision.collider.gameObject);
}
```

Code 11.5 (cont'd)

After adding these conditionals in our GameScript.cs file, restart the game by clicking the Play button. Don't forget to open the Console tab. When the RobotBoy touches a monster, the score will decrease by a random amount between 1 and 10:

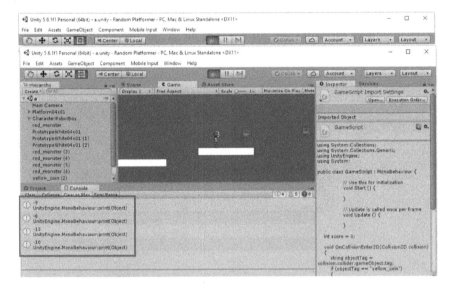

Figure 11.73. The score decreases as the RobotBoy touches monsters

We can now increase and decrease the score, great. Now, let's implement the code that will restart the level when the RobotBoy falls of the platform, in other words when the RobotBoy touches the ground. Firstly, add the required namespace by the code line using UnityEngine.SceneManagement;. Then add the following code inside the OnCollisionEnter2D method which checks if the touched object is the ground:

```
if (objectTag == "ground")
```

```
{
SceneManager.LoadScene(SceneManager.GetActiveScene().name);
}
```

Code 11.6 (cont'd)

The code line inside the condition statement reloads the scene resetting the score.

We displayed the score in the Console window using the print() method until now. However, when we distribute this game as a .exe file, the player will not play it inside the Unity but as a standalone program which won't have a Console. Therefore, it is important to show the score on the scene. The values can be displayed in a UI Text on the scene. Let's add a UI Text object by clicking the GameObject menu and then UI → Text:

Figure 11.74. Adding a UI Text on the scene

After adding the UI Text, it is better to move it to the top left of the canvas so that the score will be displayed there during the gameplay:

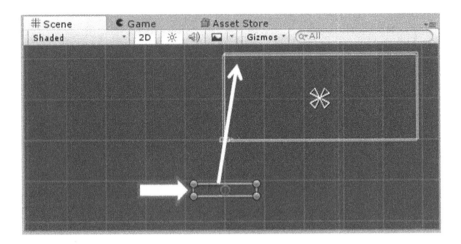

Figure 11.75. Moving the UI Text to the top left of the canvas

Now, add a tag to the UI Text as we did for various sprites before. Set the tag of the text as **scoreText**:

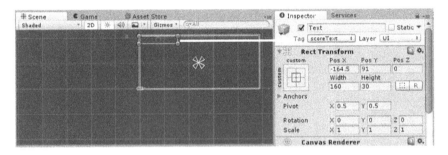

Figure 11.76. Setting the tag of the UI text

Also, change the name of the UI Text component from the hierarchy pane, set it as **scoreText**:

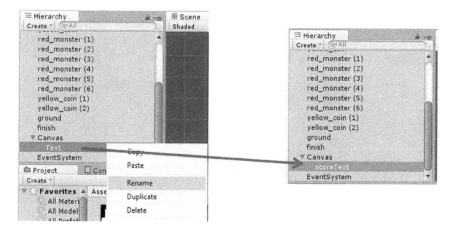

Figure 11.77. Updating the name of the UI Text

We can now access the UI Text from our C# code. We need to set the scoreText as Score: 0 in the beginning of the level. Therefore, we will place the following code inside the Start() method in the GameScript.cs file:

```
GameObject.Find("scoreText").GetComponent<Text>().text =
   "Score: " + score;
```

Code 11.7

Since the score variable is initialized to 0 in the beginning, the score will be displayed as **Score: 0** when the game starts:

Figure 11.78. The score is shown in the top left

Since the background is blue, let's change the colour of the scoreText from black to white to make it clear. We do this by selecting the scoreText and setting its colour from the Inspector:

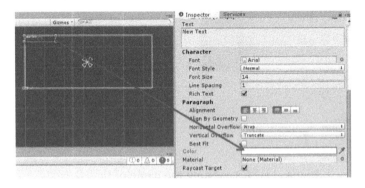

Figure 11.79. Setting the colour of the scoreText as white

Restart the game now and you will see that the score can be read easily:

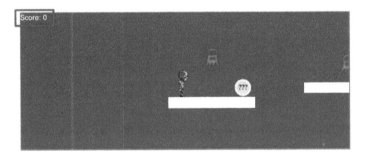

Figure 11.80. Colour of the scoreText has been changed

We need to update the scoreText when our character collides with a monster or a coin. We will add the score updating code line given in Code 16.7 inside the **if statements**:

```
if (objectTag == "yellow_coin")
{
    int randomIncrement = UnityEngine.Random.Range(1, 5);
    score = score + randomIncrement;
    print(score);
    GameObject.Find("scoreText").GetComponent<Text>().text =
                    "Score: " + score;
```

```
    Destroy(collision.collider.gameObject);

}
if (objectTag == "red_monster")
{
    int randomDecrement = UnityEngine.Random.Range(1, 10);
    score = score - randomDecrement;
    print(score);
    GameObject.Find("scoreText").GetComponent<Text>().text =
            "Score: " + score;
    Destroy(collision.collider.gameObject);
}
```

Code 11.8 (cont'd)

Click the Play button to run the game after these additions. You'll see that the score is successfully updated and displayed as our character touches monsters or collects coins:

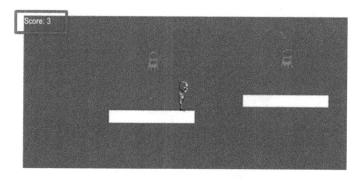

Figure 11.81. The score is shown on the top left of the scene

The only thing remaining is displaying the **Level complete!** message when the character manages to touch the green finish flag. Since we have already set its tag as **finish**, we can check if the character touches the finish line by a simple if statement:

```
if (objectTag == "finish")
{

}
```

245

Code 11.9

We will write the necessary code to show a **Level Complete** text on the screen inside this statement. For this, add a new UI Text from the GameObject menu and rename it as **levelCompleteText**:

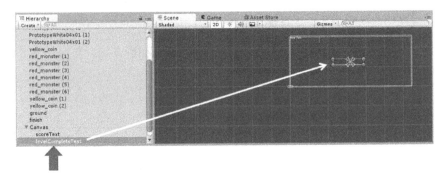

Figure 11.82. levelCompleteText on the canvas

Please position this UI Text in the middle of the canvas so that it will be shown in the middle of the screen when the level is completed. Let's increase the font size of this text to 56 units and change its colour to white. Also, set the horizontal and vertical alignments to middle from the Inspector:

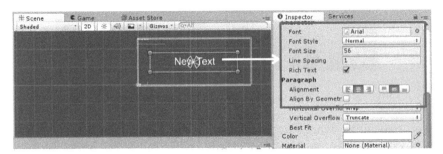

Figure 11.83. Setting the font properties of the new UI Text

When we start the game, we will see that our new UI Text appears in the middle:

Figure 11.84. The new UI Text in the middle of the scene

We don't want out level complete text to be displayed until the level is completed, i.e. until RobotBoy touches the finish sprite. Therefore, we will set the levelCompleteText as empty in the Start() method of our GameScript.cs file. We'll add the code line:

```
GameObject.Find("levelCompleteText").GetComponent<Text>()
        .text = "";
```

Code 11.10

into the Start() method:

```
void Start ()
{
GameObject.Find("scoreText").GetComponent<Text>()
        .text = "Score: " + score;
GameObject.Find("levelCompleteText").GetComponent<Text>()
        .text = "";
}
```

Code 11.11

When we restart the game now, we'll not see the new UI Text on the screen but only the score text on the top left as in Figure 11.85.

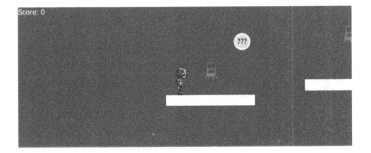

Figure 11.85. The new UI Text is invisible

As we have stated before, when RobotBoy touches the **finish** sprite, this will mean that the level is completed and the levelCompleteText will be displayed accordingly. We will implement this inside the **if** statement shown in Code 11.9.

When the RobotBoy touches the **finish** flag:

- The gravity of the RobotBoy will be removed so that he'll stay attached to the green flag.
- The **Level Complete!** text will be shown in the middle of the screen.
- The level will restart after a delay of 5 seconds which will give enough time to see the final score.

These will be done with the following code lines inside the if condition:

```
if (objectTag == "finish")
{
  GetComponent<Rigidbody2D>().gravityScale = 0.0f;
  GameObject.Find("levelCompleteText").GetComponent<Text>()
          .text = "Level Complete!";
  StartCoroutine(restartLevel());
}
```

Code 11.12

In the first line, the RigifBody2D, RobotBoy, is accessed and its gravity is nulled. In the second line, the levelCompletexText is accessed and its text is set as **Level Complete!** In the last line, a coroutine named restartLevel() is called so that the restartLevel() method will be executed in another thread. We can declare this method as follows:

```
public IEnumerator restartLevel()
{
    yield return new WaitForSeconds(5f);
    SceneManager.LoadScene(SceneManager.GetActiveScene()
                .name);
}
```

Code 11.13

In the first line, the method WaitForSeconds(5f) is called which makes the game to pause for 5 seconds. The second line restarts the level after this delay is finished.

We have now completed the C# code in which we implemented our game logic. The complete GameScript.cs is also given below for your convenience (remember that you can also download the whole project folder from the book's website):

```
using System.Collections;
using System.Collections.Generic;
using UnityEngine;
using System;
using UnityEngine.SceneManagement;
using UnityEngine.UI;
public class GameScript : MonoBehaviour
{
 void Start()
  {
    GameObject.Find("scoreText").GetComponent<Text>()
            .text = "Score: " + score;

    GameObject.Find("levelCompleteText").GetComponent
                <Text>().text = "";
  }
 void Update()
  {

  }
 int score = 0;
 void OnCollisionEnter2D(Collision2D collision)
   {
```

```
string objectTag = collision.collider.gameObject.tag;
if (objectTag == "yellow_coin")
  {
    int randomIncrement = UnityEngine.Random.Range(1, 5);
    score = score + randomIncrement;
    print(score);
    GameObject.Find("scoreText").GetComponent
             <Text>().text = "Score: " + score;
    Destroy(collision.collider.gameObject);


  }
if (objectTag == "red_monster")
  {
    int randomDecrement = UnityEngine.Random.Range(1, 10);
    score = score - randomDecrement;
    print(score);
    GameObject.Find("scoreText").GetComponent
             <Text>().text = "Score: " + score;
    Destroy(collision.collider.gameObject);
  }
if (objectTag == "ground")
  {
    SceneManager.LoadScene(SceneManager.GetActiveScene()
             .name);
  }
if (objectTag == "finish")
  {
    GetComponent<Rigidbody2D>().gravityScale = 0.0f;
    GameObject.Find("levelCompleteText").GetComponent
             <Text>().text = "Level Complete!";
    StartCoroutine(restartLevel());
  }
 }

public IEnumerator restartLevel()
 {
  yield return new WaitForSeconds(5f);
  SceneManager.LoadScene(SceneManager
             .GetActiveScene().name);
 }
}
```

Code 11.14 (cont'd)

We can now play the completed game by clicking the Play button in Unity. Although the game is simple for now, we can add new levels for a better gaming experience using the concepts we learned in this chapter.

11.5. Adding Touch Controls

We can play our game inside Unity using the arrow keys and the space bar, great. However we will not have these controls on an Android device and need to set up touch controls for this.

A simple but effective touch control scheme is to make our RobotBoy advance when the user taps the right side of the screen and to make him jump in case of the taps on the left side on the screen.

Setting up touch controls is easy in Unity. We will check the screen taps in each update of the screen therefore we will write the following code inside the Update() method of the GameScript.cs file:

```
void Update()
{
  if (Input.touchCount > 0)
  {

    Touch touch = Input.GetTouch(0);
    if (touch.position.x > Screen.width/2)
    {

      GetComponent<Rigidbody2D>().AddForce(new
          Vector2(180.0f, 0));

    }
    if (touch.position.x < Screen.width / 2)
    {
      GetComponent<Rigidbody2D>().AddForce(new
          Vector2(0, 40.0f));
    }
  }
}
```

Code 11.15

In this code snippet, the screen taps are checked in each screen update. If there is a tap (meaning that `Input.touchCount > 0`), the touch position is compared against the condition `Screen.width/2`. If `touch.position.x > Screen.width/2` is true, this means that the user tapped the right half of the screen and the RobotBoy will advance to the right with the code line:

```
GetComponent<Rigidbody2D>().AddForce(new Vector2(180.0f, 0));
```

On the other hand, if `touch.position.x < Screen.width / 2` is satisfied, this means that the user tapped the left portion of the screen and then the RobotBoy will jump by the code line:

```
GetComponent<Rigidbody2D>().AddForce(new Vector2(0, 40.0f));
```

We are now ready to export our game as an .apk file.

11.6. Exporting the Game as a Standalone .apk File

We developed our Random Platformer and can play it inside Unity. However, we have to be able to distribute the game as an .apk file so that any gamer can play it on an Android device. Exporting our game is straightforward in Unity. For this, click File → Build Settings:

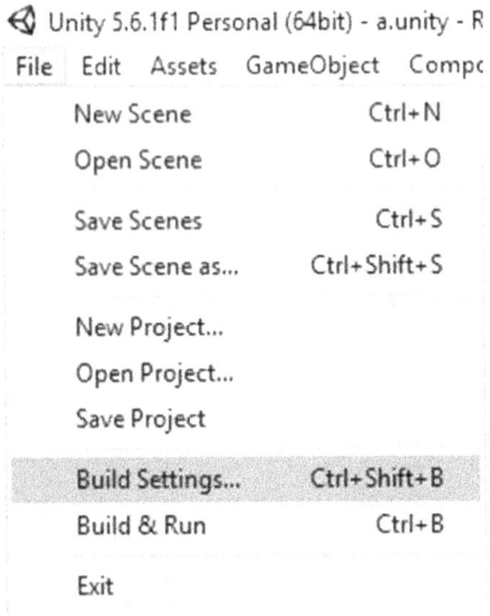

Figure 11.86. Launching the Build Settings dialog

In the dialog, select the Platform as **Android** and then click the Build button:

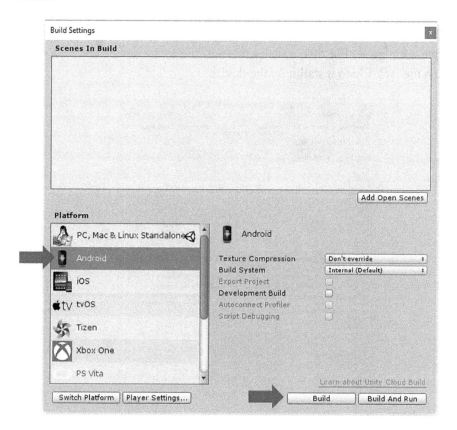

Figure 11.87. Build settings

When we click the Build button, Unity shows a file saving dialog. Specify where you want to save the .apk game on your computer and give a name for the file in this dialog. Then Unity will ask where the Android SDK root folder is. Select the Android root folder on your computer (SDK is automatically installed when Android Studio is installed). Generally, it will be at the location: C:\Users**your username**\AppData\Local\Android\sdk. Select this folder and then Unity may ask for the JDK (Java Development Kit) folder. If it is not installed on your computer, please navigate to Java download page (http://www.oracle.com/technetwork/java/javase/downloads/index.html) and then download the one suitable for your operating system as shown in Figure 11.88. After you install the JDK using the downloaded file, it will be in a folder such as C:\Program Files\Java\jdk-xxx. Select this folder and then Unity will generate the game file Random Platformer.apk as shown in Figure 11.89. We can now install it on an Android device to play our game. For this, transfer this apk file to the device and then click on the .apk file to install it on the device.

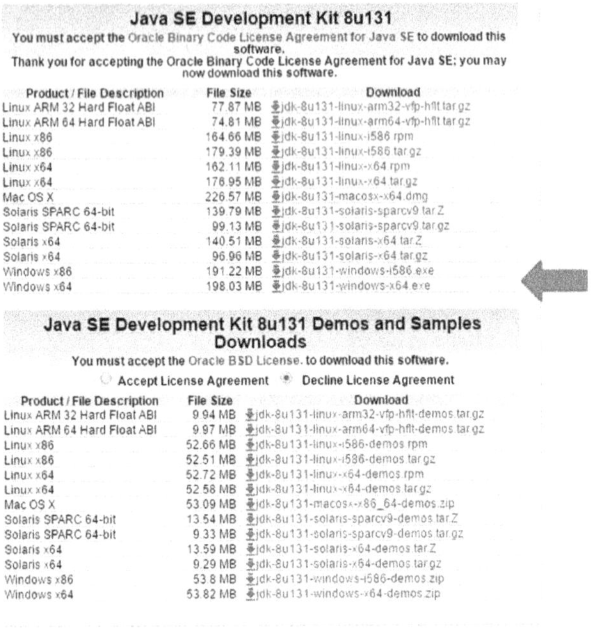

Figure 11.88. Downloading JDK

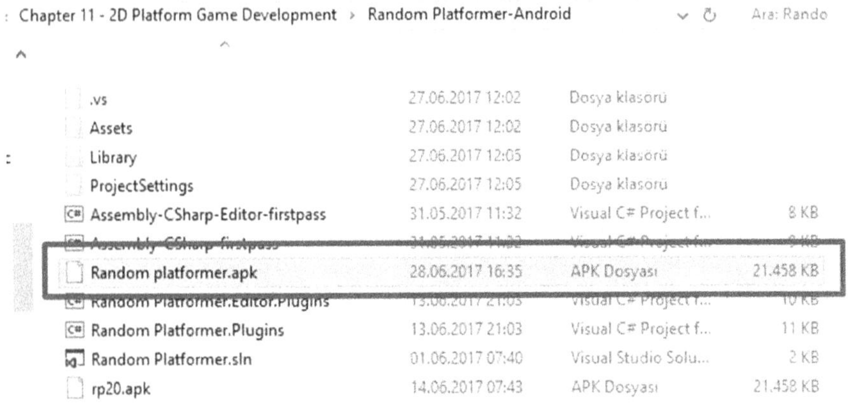

Figure 11.89. The generated .apk file of the game

We can also try this .apk file in the emulator. Please run the Android emulator from Android Studio as we in the previous projects and then drag&drop the Random Platformer.apk file on the emulator window. The .apk file will be installed automatically. Then find the Random Platformer in the programs in the emulator and click to run it. Note that you may have to change the screen orientation from the emulator options as usual. The game will start normally in the emulator. You can use clicks as screen touches in the emulator to try the game:

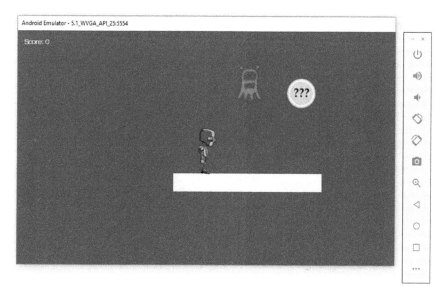

Figure 11.90. Playing our Random Platformer game in the emulator

It is now time to play the game to see is we can have the highest score possible, which is 15 (can you see why the highest score is 15?).

We have learned the basics of game development in Unity in this chapter. We can add new levels and extend our Random Platformer to make it a full game, or we can develop similar 2D games with our current Unity and Android knowledge, of course we will need to learn more C# programming to implement more complex game logic. Remember that we are only bounded with our imagination limits in the programming world!

EPILOGUE AND FUTURE WORK

I really hope that you enjoyed this book and got some confidence for developing Android apps. If you would like to share your complaints and suggestions, please feel free to drop me an e-mail at syamacli@gmail.com or share them publicly on the comments section of the book's website www.yamaclis.com/android.

This book was intended to be a starter's guide. If you have followed this book thoroughly, you should be ready to learn more on Android app development and the first source for this is, of course, the Internet. I recommend the following websites for advanced subjects:

- https://www.tutorialspoint.com/android/
- https://www.raywenderlich.com/category/android
- https://www.youtube.com/playlist?list=PLB03EA9545DD188C3

I'd like to finish this book with the following quotes which I think have deep meanings:

> "Experience is the teacher of all things."

Julius Caesar

> "To us is given the honor of striking a blow for freedom which will live in history and in the better days that lie ahead men will speak with pride of our doings."

Bernard Law Montgomery

> You cannot teach a man anything, you can only help him find it within himself.

Galileo Galilei

——— Password for the compressed files on the next page ———

REFERENCES

1. https://developer.android.com/index.html

2. https://www.udacity.com/course/android-development-for-beginners--ud837

3. http://www.instructables.com/id/How-To-Create-An-Android-App-With-Android-Studio/

4. http://www.androidauthority.com/android-studio-tutorial-beginners-637572/

5. https://www.codecademy.com/learn/learn-java

6. https://www.tutorialspoint.com/java/

7. Joseph Annuzzi Jr., Lauren Darcey and Shane Conder, Introduction to Android Application Development: Android Essentials, Addison-Wesley Professional, 2013.

8. Neil Smyth, Android Studio Development Essentials, CreateSpace Independent Publishing Platform, 2016.

9. Sam Key, Android Programming in a Day, CreateSpace Independent Publishing Platform, 2015.

10. Barry A. Burd, Android Application Development All-in-One For Dummies, For Dummies, 2015.

Password for the compressed figure and project files downloaded from the book's website www.yamaclis.com/android: 27A60

──────────── Keep calm because it's the end ☺ ────────────